My Most Memorable Encounter with God

edited by David Enlow

Tyndale
House
Publishers, Inc.
Wheaton,
Illinois

*Library
of Congress
Catalog
Card Number
77–072442
ISBN
0–8423–4655–4,
paper*
Copyright © 1977
by Tyndale House
Publishers, Inc.,
*Wheaton,
Illinois.
All rights
reserved.
First printing,
September 1977
Printed in the
United States
of America*

DAVID ENLOW

HUDSON TAYLOR ARMERDING

WILLIAM R. BRIGHT

ROBERT A. COOK

ARTHUR S. DEMOSS

EDITH EDMAN

ARMIN R. GESSWEIN

VERNON C. GROUNDS

CARL F. H. HENRY

DAVID M. HOWARD

TORREY M. JOHNSON

HAROLD LINDSELL

W. STANLEY MOONEYHAM

HAROLD JOHN OCKENGA

STEPHEN F. OLFORD

ALAN REDPATH

GEORGE BEVERLY SHEA

CLYDE W. TAYLOR

KENNETH N. TAYLOR

W. IAN THOMAS

LARRY WARD

CONTENTS

LL believers
in Jesus Christ have at least one thing in common: an
experience of conversion that begins with repentance and
confession and culminates in regeneration initiated and
completed by God Himself. But that is not all.

If the experience is genuine, leading to assurance of
everlasting life and a present reality of victory midst testings
and trials, then at least one other factor should characterize
each believer: *Some incident in the life that so obviously and
unmistakably comes from God that in no way could it be attributed
to anything or anyone else.*

The chapters of this book concern just such incidents or
experiences. They are contributed by twenty well-known
Christian men and women who have responded to my
invitation to share these important high points in their lives.

Not only will these experiences prove valuable in
strengthening your faith, but they will also be likely to
bring to mind encounters with God in your own life that
have indeed been memorable, now that you are encouraged
to recall them. This spiritual exercise will delight you and
help others who will observe your new-found joy in the
Lord.

If the world today needs "proof" of the authenticity of
the Christian experience, it needs look no further than the
true stories recounted here. Personal experience
authenticates itself; one can hardly argue with the facts. And
you will quickly recognize the spiritual authority resident in
the experiences of these twenty writers.

My grateful thanks to each of them and to Tyndale House
for a project rich in spiritual rewards to compiler-editor and
reader alike.

—David Enlow, Wheaton, Illinois

HUDSON TAYLOR ARMERDING

is the fifth president of Wheaton College. An alumnus of Wheaton, he returned to the College in 1961 as professor of history. He served as provost from February 1963 until his inauguration in January 1965. Previously he was dean and acting president of Gordon College,

Wenham, Mass., where he also taught history.

Dr. Armerding graduated cum laude in 1941 with a B.A. in history. He earned his M.A. in international affairs at Clark University and received his Ph.D. at the University of Chicago. He also has done graduate work at Harvard University. He was awarded a doctor of divinity degree by Gordon-Conwell Theological Seminary and a doctor of laws degree by Houghton (N.Y.) College.

Formerly president of the National Association of Evangelicals, Dr. Armerding is president of the World Evangelical Fellowship. He is a member of the Board of Trustees of Columbia Bible College and of the home council of Overseas Missionary Fellowship.

He holds membership in Phi Gamma Mu, Phi Kappa Delta, Wheaton College Scholastic Honor Society, Officers Christian Union, the American Legion, and the United States Naval Institute. He edited *Christianity and the World of Thought,* published by Moody Press.

A former member of the United States Naval Reserve, Dr. Armerding served as Commander of the Naval Reserve Officers school at the U.S. Armed Forces Center in Forest Park, Ill.

Christ on Our Cruiser *Hudson Taylor Armerding*

The Memorial Student Center on the Wheaton
College campus is dedicated to those who gave
their lives for their country in World War II. As
one who served in that conflict, I seldom enter
the Center without being reminded that I
survived only because of God's providential care.

The fact that God is able to preserve us even
in difficult or dangerous circumstances was one of
the convictions that governed the lives of my
godly parents. Both from Scripture and from
experience they had learned this truth. As a
missionary in Central America my father had his
life threatened by a hostile mob and later was
rescued from the jungle when he was critically ill
with malaria. In these and other ways God taught
him that He was able to sustain His servants in
critical circumstances.

My father and mother were serving the Lord
in Albuquerque, New Mexico, when I was born
into the family. They had limited financial
resources. Frequently they had to ask the Lord
for the provision of food and clothing. When I
became very seriously ill due to complications
resulting from pneumonia, they trusted God for
my recovery. Some years later on a desert
highway in California, God preserved all of us in
the family from almost certain death in an
automobile accident.

In this context of trust in God and the
experience of His faithfulness, my parents
commended me to the Lord as I entered the

United States Navy in August of 1942. After my Officer Candidate training I was assigned to the U.S.S. *Wichita,* a heavy cruiser. This ship was to be involved in eleven major engagements while I was aboard. The Lord would on these occasions frequently bring to mind this promise from Psalm 121: "The Lord shall preserve thy going out and thy coming in from this time forth and even forever more."

Although my regular duties involved the gunnery department, my battle station was in the Combat Information Center. This was the location in the ship where the tactical information from the various radars and radio circuits was assembled, interpreted, and then communicated to the commanding officer and key members of his staff. I considered myself unusually fortunate to be assigned to CIC, where we had full information about what was happening during a particular maneuver or action.

As a heavy cruiser, the *Wichita* was involved in a variety of combat operations. During several landings on the Pacific Islands the ship provided bombardment support for the troops making the assault. One of the most common assignments, however, was to serve as an anti-aircraft defense for aircraft carriers. Frequently we became part of a fast carrier task force that usually included four large carriers plus an assortment of cruisers, battleships, and destroyers in concentric rings around the carriers.

These task forces often operated at high speed and displayed intricate maneuvers when the formations changed course and the ship positions were altered. At night, the formation was completely blacked out to reduce the possibility of detection by submarines. On these occasions, orders came to the formation by short-range, high frequency radio. Radar kept the ships at appropriate distances from one another.

After some months aboard the *Wichita* I qualified as officer of the deck. During his time on watch, the officer of the deck is in charge of the ship. Intensive on-the-job training prepared an officer for this position. He served on the bridge where he could give orders to the helmsman and the engine room and could initiate announcements to the entire ship over its public address system. Reports from the various areas of the ship flowed in to the officer of the deck for his information and guidance. The commanding officer of the ship approved the assignment of his officers to this important position and they, while on watch, acted as his direct representative in exercising authority.

My watch time was shared between the bridge and the Combat Information Center. One night in the CIC, I experienced my most memorable encounter with God's providential preservation and care.

Blacked out, our ships steamed forth in a fast carrier task force. Frequent changes of course marked a zigzag plan designed to confuse enemy submarines. Periodically the flagship gave order for the entire formation to change to a new course or to a new zigzag plan.

Part way through the watch, the flagship ordered via TBS (the high frequency, short-range radio) a new zigzag plan at a specified time. The information was given in code to avoid any possibility that the transmission might be overheard and understood by the enemy.

When we had deciphered the message, I called the bridge on a voice communications system to report my understanding of the signal. A close

friend of mine was officer of the deck for that
watch. He responded by saying that he disagreed
with my interpretation of the signal. Since he
was, in effect, in command of the ship, I was in
no position to insist that he accept my point of
view.

Within a very few moments the signal came
from the flagship via radio to execute the change.
As the rest of the formation turned to the new
course, the *Wichita* continued on its previous
heading. Once again I called the bridge to warn
the officer of the deck. He still refused to accept
my opinion. Since it was my responsibility to
advise him of the radar information, I kept
reporting to the bridge the change in the
distance between the *Wichita* and the carrier on
our port beam. It had been 2,000 yards. Then it
was 1,500 yards; then 1,000 yards. It was
obvious that the carrier was heading directly for
the *Wichita.* Unless something happened, the
other ship would cut us in two.

Soon the range became so short that we could
no longer distinguish it on the radar equipment.
It would have been natural at that point to
become fraught with terror and to run from CIC
for refuge in another part of the ship. Yet,
strangely enough, this was not my reaction.

I experienced a remarkable sense of peace and
an assurance that everything would be all right.
Later I found out what happened aboard the
other ship.

The officer of the deck on the other vessel,
following standard procedure, used his binoculars
to try to see the shapes of the other ships as the
formation changed course. Despite the darkness,
it was sometimes possible to detect the outline of
another vessel. At that time of the night,
however, he also needed to depend upon his

CIC. His problem was complicated by the fact that it takes a considerable distance to stop a large vessel the size of a carrier.

Even with the limitations of visibility and distance, the other ship's officer of the deck quickly ascertained that his vessel was about to ram ours. He immediately ordered his engine room to go to full speed astern, then sounded the alarm for the closing of the watertight doors on the carrier. Yet the momentum of the carrier continued to carry it closer and closer to the *Wichita.*

Our ship's doctor was sleeping in a stateroom on the main deck and on the port side of our ship. Because the weather was warm, he had opened the porthole to get some fresh air. Suddenly he awakened. Arising, he looked out of the porthole. There against the starlit sky he saw the enormous shape of the carrier just a short distance from the side of the *Wichita.* Immediately he rushed into the Combat Information Center to find out what was happening. From his testimony we knew that we were within a few yards of being struck by the carrier and sunk. Had the carrier proceeded to hit us, the bow would have gone right through the CIC area where we were.

Recognizing at last that he was in error, my friend on the bridge brought the *Wichita* to the correct course and with the help of CIC got our ship back to the proper place in the formation.

Despite the years that have passed since that night in the western Pacific, the incident is vividly clear in my memory. I shall never forget the dramatic distinction between that which was natural and that which was supernatural. By training and experience I knew we were in mortal danger. Yet the Lord seemed to say with

quiet assurance, "Surely I will be with thee."
The sense of peace and security was not because
of the circumstances but because of His presence
in that room that was so filled with tension and
apprehension.

In a practical way I learned the truth of this
Scripture: "In all these things we are more than
conquerors through Him that loved us." It was
in this circumstance that I found Him to be
sufficient.

WILLIAM R. BRIGHT, founder and president of Campus Crusade for Christ International, was born October 19, 1921, in Coweta, Oklahoma. He is a graduate of Oklahoma Northeastern State College where he majored in economics.

Subsequent to his graduation from college, Dr.

Bright taught at Oklahoma State University, a position he later resigned to engage in several business enterprises in California, including his own manufacturing company, Bright's California Confections.

In 1946, Dr. Bright enrolled for graduate work at Princeton Theological Seminary, but continued to operate his business in California. He later transferred to Fuller Theological Seminary, where he continued his studies through the spring of 1951. While still lacking only a few units for graduation, he felt a definite leading of God to leave seminary and, rather than be ordained, to undertake a ministry which would help to reach the collegiate world for Christ. Later that year, he and his wife, the former Vonette Zachary, launched the ministry of Campus Crusade for Christ at the University of California at Los Angeles.

In 1961, the secular National University of Korea conferred upon Dr. Bright the honorary degree of Doctor of Laws for "the meritorious contributions to the development of human culture and the development of world peace through the establishment of Campus Crusade for Christ." In 1966, John Brown University honored him with the degree of Doctor of Divinity, and in 1971, Houghton College conferred upon him the honorary degree of Doctor of Letters.

Dr. Bright is the author of numerous articles, pamphlets, and two books: *Revolution Now!*, published in 1969, and *Come Help Change the World*, published in 1970.

A Vision for the World
William R. Bright

As I stepped to the microphone at EXPLO '74,
an International Student Congress on Evangelism
in Seoul, Korea, sponsored by Campus Crusade
for Christ, I surveyed a crowd of an estimated
one and a half million people. I saw scores of
photographers, reporters, and interpreters
crowded about the platform, eagerly working at
their various jobs. Distinguished Christian leaders
from many parts of the world gathered to
participate in this unprecedented event—the
largest recorded meeting in the history of the
church. This demonstration of God's Spirit
deeply moved me.

Yet, as I looked over this tremendous miracle
of God, I could not help but remember an
evening far less spectacular some twenty-four
years before. It was an evening when, far from a
large crowd, my only interested listener was my
wife, Vonette. But that evening I experienced *my
most memorable encounter with God,* apart from
receiving Christ Himself.

The setting was not conducive to "visions" or
"encounters." It was almost midnight, in the
spring of 1951, during the final semester of my
senior year of seminary, and I was studying for a
Greek exam with a classmate. We sat at a desk in
our living room. Nothing unusual marked the
setting or the circumstances. Vonette slept in a
nearby room. But suddenly I sensed the presence
of God in a way I had never known before. . . .

It is difficult to talk about such things for fear

of being misunderstood or causing others to seek after a similar experience. But the fact remains: this was the greatest spiritual moment of my Christian life. God in a supernatural way seemed to open up my mind, to give me a vision which embraced the whole world. It was so intoxicating that I almost burst with joy. I wanted to shout the praises of God at the top of my voice. I have at least a little appreciation for the experience of the apostle Paul who spoke of being lifted to a spiritual plane which could not be described by mere human words.

At this time and in a very definite way, God commanded me to invest my life in helping to fulfill the Great Commission in this generation. He impressed me to begin by helping to disciple the students of the world for Christ. How to do this was not spelled out in detail; that came later as the Lord gave additional insights for the implementation of the original vision. When I tried to tell my friend what had happened, he did not understand, though he was very sympathetic and rejoiced with me. After he had gone, I awakened Vonette. Together we praised God for His direction and promised that with His grace and strength we would obey Him.

Even with our prayer, we realized that we faced a monumental task. As I made the difficult decision to leave seminary in order to follow God's leading, Vonette and I set out alone with no well-defined plan, no financial backing for an organization, no roster of potential volunteers— not even a name for our venture. (That name, Campus Crusade for Christ, came later from Dr. Wilbur Smith of Fuller Theological Seminary. He had greeted my proposal with the confirmation, "This is of God.")

Vonette and I felt a lack in our own "spiritual

maturity" and experience in working with college students. An agnostic and skeptic through college and the beginnings of my business career, I had received Christ as my personal Savior only a few years before. Vonette, who had once declared that she would marry me only if she could rescue me from this "religious fanaticism," had instead dedicated her life to Christ during our engagement. But that was also little more than two years before.

Since our marriage, we had been involved in our local church—primarily in a deputation group to jails and skid row missions. Efforts with college students had been singularly unsuccessful. In spite of all these things, we did have a strong desire to make our lives count for Christ. This was expressed in a "contract" we signed together with God, in which we relinquished all claims on our lives.

In our home in the Hollywood hills, Vonette went into one room and I into another. We made a list of all the things we had wanted out of life. When I had first proposed to Vonette, as a young businessman, we both had luxurious, expensive appetites. We enjoyed the good life. We had talked about a honeymoon in Europe, about securing the finest voice teacher to develop her beautiful singing voice, and about living in the fabulous Bel Air district of Los Angeles. But now all that had been given to Christ. Such ambitions had become secondary, if not non-existent (not that they are wrong goals in themselves, but for us there was no longer a great appetite for them). So, we made a new list of the things we wanted.

Our new lists, surprisingly alike, included: 1) to live holy lives, controlled and empowered by the Holy Spirit; 2) to be fruitful in our witness for Christ; and 3) to help fulfill the Great Commission in our generation.

The commitment of our home to Christ proved to be a focal point in the early days of the ministry—one of the most obvious ways that God confirmed our decision. After seeking counsel from more mature Christians (the first board of directors included Dr. Wilbur Smith, Dr. Henrietta Mears, Billy Graham, Dick Halverson, Dawson Trotman, Cy Nelson, Dan Fuller, and Edwin Orr) and deciding on UCLA as a place to begin, the next step was to find a house to live in near the campus. Rents were high and nothing was readily available, but I noticed a listing for a large house only one block from the campus.

When the realtor flipped the card to the listing of this house, I told him rather emphatically, "*That's the house.* I want to see it."

"Why?" he asked. "They are asking more than twice the amount you are willing to pay."

But I continued to press him. "How long has the house been listed?"

"For several months." Then he explained how two sisters who lived in the house planned to take a South American tour. "As a matter of fact," he observed, studying the card, "they leave next week."

After asking permission to go to see them, we found the house ideally suited to our needs. I explained to the owners our interest in reaching the students of UCLA for Christ. We would not be able to pay more than half the monthly rent they were requesting. They said they would think about it and would call us. By the time I returned to our home in Hollywood, they had called. Shortly thereafter we moved into our new home in Westwood.

With a home base, Vonette and I organized a twenty-four-hour prayer chain among church members with the single request that God would "do a unique thing on the UCLA campus." Next we began to recruit students to join us in visiting fraternities and sororities, dormitories and other groups—explaining to their fellow students who Christ is, why He came and how they could know Him personally.

I remember well our first sorority meeting. At the conclusion, I was amazed to see such a large group of young women standing in line to express their desire to become Christians. One after another they came (more than half of the original girls present), communicating in various ways, "I want to become a Christian."

For more than a year we had gone into various fraternity and sorority houses on local campuses prior to the time God gave the vision for this ministry; yet we had never seen one single person commit his life to Christ. Now we had a dramatic confirmation that the plan to reach the students of the world truly came from God.

Within a few months, more than 250 students—including the student body president, the editor of the newspaper and a number of top athletes—committed their lives to Christ. Other colleges and universities began to ask us to start the same kind of movement on their campuses. Since Vonette and I could not duplicate ourselves, we began to recruit a staff. At first we had only six young men who received salaries of $100 a month for only nine months of the year.

As I look back on our beginning days, I often think of the vision that God gave me that memorable night as the beginning strokes on a giant-size painting. The artist with bold, broad strokes paints the landscapes, the mountains.

Later he fills in the details. Had God given me all of the details that night, I am sure I would have lost my sanity. I could not possibly have endured it. But He gave me what I could handle, and that was an experience never to be forgotten.

Had that vision lived fresh and vividly in my memory day after day, I would have been unable to survive. So God just rolled it back and I began to start small—one-to-one with students—working on one campus, UCLA. And I was happy there. I didn't forget the vision, but it was in the back of my mind.

Over the years God has filled in many of the details of the initial vision. From our beginning at UCLA, we moved to San Diego State, University of Southern California, University of California at Berkeley, Oregon State, and the University of Washington the following year. By 1956, our staff had grown to the point of needing new summer training facilities. In the fall of that year, a long distance call from Mound, Minnesota, resulted in the gift of five acres of land on the shores of Lake Minnetonka—and we moved to a new training center. Soon this beautiful facility was no longer large enough.

In 1961, God's remarkable provision led us to yet another headquarters—Arrowhead Springs, California. Hollywood film stars had built this beautiful resort and hotel, once a vacation spot for the wealthy and famous of the world.

By this time our staff had grown to 109 with ministries on forty campuses in fifteen states. We also had staff members in Korea and Pakistan, and had just begun to produce a weekly radio program on several stations.

With this desperate need for new facilities in

mind and the knowledge that the California property was available at a "greatly reduced price" of $2,000,000 (an incredible amount for our organization, which had never had an extra dollar in its ten years of existence), I went to see the property. As I knelt in the quiet, beautiful, old hotel, I prayed, "I am overwhelmed, Lord. This place is so big and beautiful. True, we've been asking you to direct us to large, new facilities, but if this is it, where will we get the money to buy it? It seems too impossible even to consider. Yet, I keep hearing in my heart Your voice, and it suggests that this is the place You want us to have. If it is, then You are going to have to make it crystal clear. How can I know for sure?"

Then, though not in an audible voice, God spoke to me as clearly as if there had been a public address system in the room. Unmistakably I heard Him say, "I have been saving this for Campus Crusade for Christ. I want you to have it, and I will supply the funds to pay for it."

With tears running down my face, I said, "God, I don't know how You intend to work this miracle, but I know You can, and I thank You for this gift. I claim this property in Your name."

Then began the amazing series of circumstances which eventually brought the international headquarters of Campus Crusade for Christ to Arrowhead Springs—another step in the fulfillment of the vision. Every financial move proved a precarious one for months—indeed, for the first several years. But we were never late in making a single payment.

The most dramatic deadline, however, was the final one—the accumulation of the complete $2,000,000. An unusual offer from Guy F.

Atkinson, a leading builder of multimillion-dollar construction projects, precipitated that day. After carefully checking the operations and policies of Campus Crusade, he offered to give us $300,000 if the balance of the debt were raised within one year from that day. It was an exciting challenge, and yet twelve months later on the evening of the deadline, when every source of revenue had been exhausted (including the sale of some land), we still needed $33,000.

At about 10 P.M., with two hours to go before the deadline, Vonette and I knelt with our two sons, Zachary and Bradley. We prayed with a new urgency. I prayed first, then Vonette and then Zac. But it was Brad's prayer that I remember. He was only seven years old, but he spoke to the heart of the matter: "Lord, we need this money and we ask You to send it right away."

After praying and putting the boys to bed, I reached for my Bible and discovered a slip of paper which I had brought home from the office and forgotten. On it was the name and phone number of a man who, when I returned his call, offered to give $5,000. After this impressive start, I remembered an attorney who had offered $17,000 to buy a piece of land that had been donated to Campus Crusade. I called to offer the property for $22,000. He countered with an $18,000 offer for the land, and the needed funds were now down to $10,000.

In the meantime, members of the staff gathered in the hotel lobby to pray. A successful Arizona businessman, Arlis Priest, who had generously taken a year from his business to help us, recalls the evening: "It was getting late. My wife, Nadine, and I were both in bed when some of the staff began to knock at our door.

This happened several times. Each time someone would hand me an envelope with money in it. The first few I looked at were $25, $100 and $150. A peace came over me, for I knew God was doing something special. These dedicated staff members who had hardly enough money to live on were giving the widow's mite."

With only fifteen minutes until the deadline, we were still praying for the needed $10,000. Then Dr. Walter Judd, former U.S. Congressman and medical missionary, called to offer the last $5,000 if it were needed. Shortly after that, Vonette remembered another $5,000 that had been set aside in case of a special need. A call to the property manager confirmed that the money still was available, and with a final call to Dr. Judd at two minutes before midnight, the deadline was met.

By this time, Vonette and the members of the staff and I were so excited and filled with gratitude to the Lord that we decided to meet immediately in the International Theater in the hotel to thank Him for this miracle. It was a beautiful experience. Never have I heard the doxology sung with such vigor. Never did the lyrics, "Praise God from whom all blessings flow . . ." hold so much meaning.

That was not the end of financial traumas for Arrowhead Springs. In fact, a difficulty in a land negotiation almost cost the loss of the property just ten days later. But that event did mark another confirmation of my vision many years before.

Many other confirmations and blessings have appeared over the years. We developed our own materials, such as the Four Spiritual Laws and the Holy Spirit booklet, for example. We developed a strategy for the campus ministry, later expanding it to include laymen. Then came the work with athletes, the music ministry, the high school work, a ministry to minority groups, to prisoners, and expansion to other countries. We now have almost 5,000 staff serving Christ in eighty-two countries.

Besides the more than 300,000 people who were trained in Korea at Explo '74, thousands have been trained in conferences over the years—80,000 at EXPLO '72 in Dallas, Texas, alone. Through the ministries of just two of our staff—campus speaker, Josh McDowell, and illusionist, Andre Kole—hundreds of thousands have been introduced to Jesus Christ.

These things and many more, I believe, are just the beginning. The vision God gave me was of such magnitude that I can say we have not even begun to see what I know we shall see. This is just a drop in the bucket. I am confident we shall experience a hundredfold more results than we have seen up to now. God showed me the whole world and gave me the confidence that He would use me and others in this generation to reach the multitudes of the world for whom Christ died.

Looking on the past twenty-five years since God gave me His vision, I shout His praises. It is because of my confidence in the character of God that I can face the challenge of these critical times with a joyful heart and the assurance that we shall soon see the greatest spiritual awakening of all time. I readily identify with the psalmist who wrote, "I will praise the Lord and call on all men everywhere to bless His holy name forever and forever."

DR. ROBERT A. COOK began his 15th
year as president of The King's College,
Briarcliff Manor, New York, on March 17,
1977.

A graduate of the Moody Bible Institute,
Wheaton College, and Eastern Baptist Seminary,
Dr. Cook served congregations in Philadelphia,

Pa., LaSalle, Ill., and Chicago before becoming
director of Chicagoland Youth for Christ. He
served as president of Youth for Christ
International for ten years, and for five years as
vice-president of Scripture Press, Wheaton, Ill.,
before taking the presidency of The King's
College.

Dr. Cook writes constantly for the religious
press and has authored eight books, among them
Now That I Believe. This publication, after twenty
years and sales of over 700,000 copies, was listed
as the number one in volume sales for Moody
Press paperbacks in 1971. It has been translated
into twenty-seven languages.

Dr. Cook traveled throughout the world in
evangelism crusades and Bible conferences in
connection with his work in Youth for Christ.
He is past-president of the National Association
of Evangelicals and presently serves on the
executive board and as chairman of the
Resolutions Committee of that organization. He
is a member of a number of academic
organizations and missionary boards. Dr. Cook is
married and the father of three daughters, two
married and one in college.

Dr. Cook may be heard regularly on "The
King's Hour," a radio program of The King's
College now aired over twenty-five daily radio
stations and eight weekly stations.

He Guides Our Delays
Robert A. Cook

India made a profound impression on me.

I was tired when I got there at four in the
morning. Tired from weeks of having several
meetings a day, in the Philippines, China, and
Japan. Merrill Dunlop and I thought that at long
last we must know something about how
missionaries feel just before furlough!

And now, India. We had left Haneda Airport
outside of Tokyo, touched down briefly in Hong
Kong, stopped at Bangkok where I took a
picture of a barefooted soldier with a sore toe.
As he looked sternly at me and clutched his
ancient Springfield rifle, I thought, *Well, no one is
going to steal this airport!*

The hours ground on, with the muted roar of
the engines ever in our ears. Finally, sometime
between three-thirty and four in the morning, we
touched down at Dum Dum Airport, fifteen
miles outside of Calcutta.

Forty minutes waiting finally brought the
health and immigration officers on board to
check our papers. There was the inevitable form
to fill out, with its inevitable question: "Where
did you spend the last fourteen nights?" I
wondered why they never asked about the last
fourteen *days.*

Dawn was breaking when we left the airplane
and filed into the immigration and customs
building. I remember feeling a bit nervous when
an officer waved me along with his machine gun
pointed at my equator, saying, "You're in our

country now . . . move along!" I said, "I know
it . . . but please be careful with that thing! I'm
the only me I've got!" I don't think he
understood me.

Customs took another hour. I had to leave one
suitcase with the authorities because it contained
quantities of movie film and some flash bulbs.
(Came back the next day and said to the person
in charge, "I am here to pick up the suitcase I
left with you yesterday." "Yes, sir!" he said, and
gave it to me.)

Finally, we were out into the reception area,
there to be met by Hubert Mitchell and Dick
Reilly. These two stalwarts had taken the last bus
out from the city the night before, and had
stayed in the airport all night, waiting for the
arrival of our plane. I learned later that they had
made a night-long evangelistic rally out of it,
witnessing to everyone in sight.

The ride into the city remains etched in
memory. First one had to bargain with the taxi
driver. A wise precaution, I learned, because the
meter on those ancient cabs invariably had been
altered to run up an astronomical total. "No one
goes by the meter," I was told. "You settle the
price first, before you get into the cab."

The sights, sounds, and smells along the way
were overpowering. The sacred cows occasionally
blocking our progress moved with infinite
reluctance, as though they were doing us a great
favor. The people, ah, the people! standing in
the roadway, squatting by the gutter, lying on
the sidewalk, eating a meager meal at a roadside
stand, carrying heavy burdens from here to
there, begging for the stray rupee that might fall
into their cups . . . people everywhere. I learned
from my hosts that every night many of these
same people I was seeing would die, mainly of

starvation, and would be picked up by a cart in the early morning hours, to be buried.

I began to feel a sense of numbness, of burden, of awe, of fear, of despair—something I knew could be counteracted only by prayer.

Pray I did, during those weeks Merrill Dunlop and I spent in India. Every morning before dawn I was awake, seeking God, asking for strength and power to live for my Lord. And if some days I might sleep until dawn, the sad wail of a beggar woman taking up her station on the street five stories below me would awaken me. She must have had perfect pitch, because her little song began with the same note—*A flat,* I figured.

Perhaps nowhere else in all the world have I been so aware of the need for God's presence, and for prayer that "prays through" and gets an answer. Each day was a new series of challenges involving spirit, soul, and body. The incredible poverty of the masses, the stirrings even then of godless communism, the daily evidence of satanic opposition and of demon possession in the lives of people one might meet—all of this forced me to seek God.

And God answered! Even in times when one's body was weak and ill, there was the blessed sense of His nearness. Missionaries whom we met proved as always to be the finest of human beings, truly God's nobility. Prayer meetings and evangelistic services with them always brought refreshment and delight.

In the initial culture shock, as I entered a country whose language and customs were entirely unfamiliar to me, I called upon God for the at-ease feeling that only He can give in strange circumstances. In the early morning hours, when the cry of the needy began even before the sun was up, I sought Him for strength to live another day in the face of multiplied meetings, exhausting heat, and satanic opposition. In the midnight hours, when struck by the realization that home and loved ones were twelve thousand miles away, I prayed for assurance that they, and I, would be kept in His care.

In the continuing heartbreak of seeing the misery of people—children with hunger and death in their dark eyes, the indescribable cruelty of life as a beggar, the complete isolation of the outcast, forsaken by society even though the law said it was wrong to do so, the hopelessness of those who could not ever hope for what we call a square meal—I sought the Lord to give me compassion and strength to do what one could.

I was constantly aware of the almost impossible task of the wonderful missionaries, many of them exhausted by trying to do too much with too little, and I prayed for the ability to send the help they needed. How I prayed for a new touch of gratitude and dedication to the God who meets one on the road of life, and who supplies each need according to His riches in glory.

Finally, it was time to leave. It was early morning in Calcutta, and once again we were back at the airport. The baggage was checked, the last goodbyes were said, and Merrill Dunlop and I were ready to board the plane which would take us on around the world in the direction of home.

When it came time to board, however, we were shocked to discover that neither of our names was on the passenger list. We were told quite firmly that unless we were listed on the manifest, we could not board the flight.

Protests and pleas availed nothing and the plane took off without us. Now it seemed quite certain that our connections in Europe and Great Britain would be missed and a long delay would ensue. All of this had happened in spite of very careful preparations which had included checking with the airlines office repeatedly. We had tried to take care of every last detail so that nothing would be amiss in this last leg of our long journey around the world.

There was nothing to do but to return to the city. Upon checking with the airlines office, we discovered that someone had indeed made a mistake and had inadvertently left our names off the manifest. The next available flight would not leave for two or three days.

So, we waited.

I must admit I did some complaining to God at that point. Here we were, stuck in lodgings that were anything but pleasant, being delayed just long enough to ruin all our plans for a quick return to the USA.

I remember how I pled with the airlines representative in London to put me on a flight which was leaving almost immediately for New York. With the impeccable courtesy and firmness for which the British are famous, he assured me that nothing could be done. The flight was full, and that was that. Other flights were also full, and I would have to wait my turn and leave after a wait of two or three days.

"Well," we said to each other, "since we are stuck here for another day or so, let's go over to Switzerland and see the Bible Institute at Beatenberg and say hello to Frau Dr. Wasserzug." This we did, and had a most blessed and relaxing time with God's choice servants. I bade farewell to Merrill Dunlop and headed for my delayed flight home.

Upon returning to London, I picked up a

newspaper and was shocked to see in large
headlines the account of an airplane crash in
which many had lost their lives. Reading a little
farther in the article, I discovered to my horror
that this was the plane which I had so fervently
desired to board some hours before! I stopped
where I was on that London street, bowed my
head, and thanked God that He had caused a
clerk in Calcutta to make a mistake which most
certainly had saved my life.

That whole experience, involving several
weeks, is now one great mural on the walls of
memory. In all of it I needed God as never
before, and I found Him there, ready and willing
to meet my need.

I prayed during those days in 1948, and God
answered.

Yes, I guess you could say this was one of my
most memorable encounters with God!

ARTHUR S. DEMOSS, founder, president, and chairman of the board of National Liberty Corporation of Valley Forge, Pa., pioneered in the mass marketing of insurance when, in 1959, he ran an advertisement in a weekly paper offering lower rates for health and accident insurance sold directly by mail.

From this humble beginning has grown a business which now insures almost two million Americans, is the largest mass-marketer of health and life insurance in the world, and has assets today of some $300 million.

DeMoss was born in Albany, N.Y., on October 26, 1925. Too impatient to finish a college education, he traveled across America, visiting practically every state before he reached the age of sixteen.

At the age of thirty-three, he was a successful general insurance agent, having agencies in several states. It was at this point that he began applying mass merchandising techniques to the sale of insurance and founded National Liberty.

DeMoss is chairman of the board of National Liberty Life Insurance Company, National Home Assurance Company of New York, National Independence Insurance Company, National Assets Management Corporation, National Puerto Rican Management Company, National Liberty Foundation of Valley Forge, and National Home Life Assurance Company.

He is a director of Campus Crusade for Christ International, National Liberty International Corporation, and the National Association of Life Companies. He is president of the American Business Men's Research Foundation, Inc., and is a trustee of Tennessee Temple College, and Gordon-Conwell Seminary.

He and his wife, Nancy, formerly of Charlotte, reside with their seven children in Bryn Mawr, Pennsylvania.

Friday the 13th: My "Lucky Day"
Arthur S. DeMoss

Many memorable encounters with God have been my experience these past twenty-seven years, since I first joined His great and wonderful family. Initially I found myself getting off the roller coaster existence which I had been on for so long, and getting on a permanent high with Jesus Christ. After spending so many years of my life searching in vain for thrills and excitement, every day since becoming a Christian has been thrilling and exciting.

This is true not only when things are going well, but also in times of pressure, problems, and even apparent calamities. In fact, it is here in particular when I have had some very meaningful encounters with God. He has impressed upon me this fact: now that the ultimate issue of life has been settled, everything else—whether seemingly good or bad—is relatively unimportant.

Recently, after many very good and relatively trouble-free years, I suddenly encountered a series of reverses—personal and business. First, our home caught fire in the middle of the night, with eleven of us sound asleep at the time. We were burned out, but extremely fortunate that we all escaped alive and well.

Shortly thereafter, the doctors discovered that my wife, Nancy, required extensive and delicate surgery for a serious and very large tumor at the base of her brain. While the Lord miraculously brought her through this, it was touch-and-go for a long time.

At about the same time, I found myself in the midst of some extremely heavy financial losses, amounting to many millions of dollars. Some of this may have been my own fault, but much of it came from factors over which I had no control. I also personally guaranteed a multi-million dollar transaction which went bad.

Through it all, I found God very real and very near. I learned to depend more on Him and to trust totally in Him, thus making it all a very precious and memorable experience. In fact, it has been indescribably wonderful to become so intimately related to the Lord that *every* experience of life represents a manifestation of God's grace to us.

None of this could have happened, however, had it not been for one particular encounter with the living God many years earlier. . . .

It was Friday the thirteenth, a day that made bettors at the race track go crazy. I slept until noon on this particular October day in 1950. Black cats, broken mirrors, and Friday the thirteenths didn't bother me. I was a "system" gambler. It wasn't luck to me, it was a skill—a skill made perfect by my formulas and systems.

But little did I know that before the day was out my entire life would be changed, revolutionized—not through luck or even through one of my own systems, but through simple faith in Jesus Christ.

As far back as my early teens—years earlier—I had a penchant for taking chances. Slipping away from prep school in Albany, New York, I hitchhiked all over America. I was particularly fascinated by Las Vegas where I could play my systems at the big gaming tables. Back at school, I found I could win money from the other kids—most of whom came from well-to-do families—by taking their bets at election time, particularly at so much per state or per electoral vote. I also ran football pools and stayed up late at night playing cards. I lost on occasion, but by being a student of gambling I was able to win most of the time. It seemed like an easy way to get ahead.

Before I was out of my teens, I became involved in gambling on a full-time basis. I soon found myself handling more than $10,000 a day. And this certainly wasn't conducive to my developing much of a sense of values!

Then my evenings were spent at the night clubs and gambling spots, and my mornings in bed—sleeping.

While I was satisfied with my way of life, it was a great concern to my mother. A small, vivacious and godly woman who read the Bible constantly, Mom strongly disapproved of my life style—particularly when I brazenly installed extra phones in my room upstairs and started taking horse bets right in our own home.

During all these years, my "Bible" was the Racing Form. I thought rarely, if ever, about God. But my dear mother kept praying for me—and kept prodding me. Unfortunately, I didn't understand. I thought she was trying to get me to quit sinning and to start being "good." Needless to say, I had neither the desire nor the ability.

Now, on this particular Friday the thirteenth, I got up late and went downstairs for breakfast—and my daily encounter with Mother.

"Breakfast or lunch?" she asked.

It was her usual way of letting me know she disapproved of my late hours.

"When are you going to start living like a normal person?" she asked seriously. "It was four o'clock when you got home this morning."

As Greeks, our emotions were always on the surface. I knew that by playing along, giving her a big kiss, and staying clear of an argument, I would soon have her smiling again.

Mother shrugged off my kiss. "You think only about yourself," she said. "God didn't create you to be a sponge. Why can't you be like your brother Bob?"

I laughed and patted her cheek. "Hey, isn't one seminary graduate enough in our family?"

"Don't make jokes," she said seriously. "Bob, Dora, and your three aunts are all praying for you. Besides, I've never seen your father so concerned."

I thought of that conversation I'd had with my father several years before. A business friend had come around to his jewelry shop and said, "I'm worried about your boy Arthur. He's running with a bad gang and will end up in prison unless he changes soon."

My father had come to me that evening with the same line Mother was using now. "Why can't you be like your brother? I've never seen two boys so different."

I liked being different. But the idea of all those folks praying for me was unnerving. I wolfed down my brunch and bolted for the door. If I was lucky I'd be able to catch the first race.

Daily, for the past two weeks, I had been passing a mammoth converted horse stable along the road where a huge sign announced revival meetings conducted by a Jewish Christian, Hyman Appelman. The sight of the tent always brought a chuckle as I thought of religion and horses under the same roof. That evening, though, as I returned home, for some reason I swung into the parking lot and slipped into the back of the stable. If the speaker wasn't interesting or if someone tried to put pressure on me to "get religion," I could always sneak out.

As I look back, after all these years, I can see how God sent this particular preacher to speak in a converted horse stable just to reach me for Jesus Christ. Dr. Appelman was a former lawyer. Instead of playing on the emotions, he came on like a trial lawyer presenting a case to a jury. It was probably the only approach that would have caught my interest—and held it.

Concise, logical, Dr. Appelman talked to the crowd about sin, how we were filled with it, how it separated us from God. Then he described the new life God offered. "God can forgive you and make you clean," he said. "He can give you a new start and a new life. The new life is worth more than all the money in the world."

I had heard these words, or words like them, before. But this time, for some reason, they were striking home. I felt myself leaning forward on the edge of the bench, straining to hear every word. The evangelist held up his Bible.

"Here it says very specifically that Jesus Christ came into the world to save sinners. God sent His Son into this world, not to rule as a king on a throne, but to mingle among sinners and redeem their lives. He came for *you*—don't ever get away from this fact."

My heart was pounding in my chest like fists on a hollow drum. I could feel the drops of perspiration forming in my hands. My collar was wet even though it was cool in the big old building.

"Why are we here in this world?" the preacher asked. "To live as we want to live, to do just what we want to do without responsibility to our Maker?

"God made us, He loves us, and His heart aches over the way we ignore Him. How much patience is He supposed to have? How much patience would you as a father have if your child treated you as you treat God?"

I thought of the words of my mother that morning, how she and Bob and all the others were praying for me. I thought about my father's deep concern for me. And I thought about all those empty people out at the race track, in the bars and the casinos.

The words of the evangelist were ringing in my ears. "There isn't much time. Are you willing to gamble with your soul when all eternity is at stake?"

I could hardly believe all this was happening. I had the same sensations that were present when I was standing at a roulette table, or throwing the dice on the green felt, holding my breath as two horses approached the wire neck and neck, or trying to bluff out three other fellows at a poker table. Only here the stakes were higher than ever before. Instead of winning or losing a fortune, I could lose my soul. My eternal life was hanging in the balance.

"Come," the evangelist said deliberately. "Come, and give your heart and life to Jesus Christ."

I literally exploded from the bench, rushing down the aisle into a new life. As I moved forward, I was aware of a new presence inside me. It was as though I had left the old Art DeMoss back there on the back bench in the horse stable while the new man, now filled with the presence of the living Christ, was moving forward to an unexplored but tremendously exciting promise of life.

I was back the next night, and the next. One

afternoon I had a long talk with the evangelist about my future. He told me the importance of studying the Bible which, he said, was God's handbook for life. Just as a gambler studies the systems, so I should study and learn the Word of God. His advice made a profound impression on me and I could hardly wait to get back to the house and start reading the Bible.

It was my mother who first noticed the change. When she quizzed me about it, I told her of my experience at the horse stable. She listened to me intently, almost suspiciously. She had heard so many of my stories, listened to so many promises. But this time she, too, realized I was not spoofing. I watched her eyes fill with tears and then heard her as she began to cry out, "Thank you, dear God. . . ."

My friends had a bit more trouble. "Don't worry, Art," they kidded. "You'll be your old self in a few days."

But they were wrong. My old self had been left behind in that stable. It was a new Arthur DeMoss who was now alive and walking the streets of Albany.

People ask if it was much of a struggle to give up my old habits—gambling, drinking, and my loose life. But as I began to study the Bible and spend time on my knees in prayer, I found that my desires had changed also. The old habits and pastimes simply sloughed off. Perhaps the most accurate way to describe it is in the words of the Apostle Paul: "When someone becomes a Christian he becomes a brand new person inside. He is not the same any more. A new life has begun!" (2 Cor. 5:17).

My gambling operation was replaced with a new organization I called "Missionary Evangelism, Inc."—a foundation offering help to foreign missions and mission-minded churches.

All abilities, including the ability to make money, come from God. The natural man will adulterate this ability—use it for self gain and to the detriment of others. The redeemed man, however, with the same ability, will use it for the glory of God. That's what I wanted to do.

The writer of Proverbs says, "Before every man there lies a wide and pleasant road that seems right but ends in death. . . . A wise man is cautious and avoids danger" (Prov. 14:12, 16).

Life is still a gamble. Every day now I make decisions which, if botched, could hurt not only me but many others as well. Yet God provides guidance, direction, and wisdom not of this world, which enable me not only to continue on but to love every minute of it. As an ambassador for Jesus Christ I awake each day with an excitement that the men with the green eye shades in their smoke-filled rooms never even dream about. It is the excitement of betting my life—day by day—on Jesus Christ. And knowing I can't lose!

Perhaps you can better see now why my encounter with God on that Friday the thirteenth was so memorable!

EDITH EDMAN is the widow of Dr.
V. Raymond Edman, the former president of
Wheaton College, who died in 1967. She now
lives in Salem, Oregon.

A strong believer in Bible study and prayer,
Mrs. Edman has a rich counseling ministry
among young and old alike. She has initiated

prayer groups among women wherever she has lived.

Her first mission field, with her husband, was the country of Ecuador. When his health failed, and he was led to new areas of service, Edith Edman successively and successfully became a pastor's wife, then an educator's wife.

Of special interest to Mrs. Edman is Evangelist Billy Graham, who early in his student career became her prime prayer subject. Often her day begins at 4:00 A.M. with a fruitful ministry of intercession.

Writing about her in *Power,* Gladys Hunt observed: "Edith Edman has a heart big enough to include the world and a God big enough to meet its needs. Her type of praying demands both!"

Spared to Serve
Edith Edman

Until late 1974, I would have had to point to an experience forty-six years earlier—in Guayaquil, Ecuador—as my most memorable encounter with God. And indeed even today I rejoice and praise God for what He did in my life on that eventful day almost five decades ago.

My husband, the late V. Raymond Edman, had gone to Ecuador as a missionary. In 1925, I joined him to become his bride and helpmeet in the task of bringing the gospel to the people of Ecuador.

We intended that Ecuador would be our home, that we would give our lifetime to its people. But in time God had other plans for us. Before a second year had passed, my husband almost died of typhus and we had to return to the States for an eighteen-month period of recuperation.

When we returned to Ecuador in early 1928 it was to a Bible school ministry, in which we hoped to train nationals for the work of the church. This time I saw Raymond stricken with dengue and amoebic dysentery. He became so weak that he had to teach some of his classes from his bed. When no improvement came, he was sent to the States for further care. I remained in Ecuador with the younger of our two small sons.

It was a tremendously confusing time. What could I do, one missionary alone with a child? Meanwhile, I saw such enormous needs around me. I was lonely, scared, and frustrated.

In my room in the port city of Guayaquil, I

asked God for a fresh anointing of His Spirit. I determined not to leave that room until God had proved His reality and adequacy for the situation. God showed Himself to me that day and things have not been the same since. A fresh infilling came to me. He showed me it was His work, not mine, and I had only to rest in His power and faithfulness.

This experience did not make me complacent, but zealous. It brought me to a new plateau of discipleship, an experience that has been repeated a number of times in my life.

Meanwhile, medical officials in the States would not give my husband a clean bill of health to return to the tropics. Instead, my son and I returned home to be reunited with the rest of the family. We had thought God's "anywhere" for us was Ecuador; instead, we found ourselves in a tiny pastorate in Worcester, Mass.

But God had a bigger plan in mind, though we couldn't see it immediately. For it was while we were there that Raymond earned the Ph.D. that later set him on the road to becoming a Christian educator.

At home, I had the confining experience of mothering three small children. I didn't feel much like the missionary I had set out to become. My husband was busy away from home a good deal. Yet somehow during those days, I came to read the *Memoirs of McCheyne.* Here was the account of a young Scottish clergyman who longed to see God work. McCheyne's passion for revival seemed to become mine and I was deeply stirred.

Suddenly the thought came to me: *Here I am at twenty-nine—content with only my small world.* I determined then that I would also see a mighty movement of God in my lifetime.

So I began to pray. And I started a women's prayer group, a practice I have continued wherever we have lived. Always we were led to pray that God would send a revival among His people.

When we moved, so that Raymond could join the faculty of the Nyack Missionary Training School (now Nyack College) in 1935, I prayed for revival among the students. So persistent was God's leading in that direction that I often asked my husband when he came home, "Are there any signs of revival on campus?"

I believe God put such intense praying in my heart. He wanted to make my world larger than the home, and I knew that in time He would let me see the answer to these prayers.

Years later, in 1943, three years after my husband had become president of Wheaton College, revival did break out among the students. Concern for personal holiness, for a right relationship with God and others, broke out all over campus and kept students in prayer all night. God again had answered many prayers, including mine.

One night after Raymond had finished praying with a freshman boy who had received Christ, he turned to find another young man, a senior—pastor of a local church—seeking the Lord's anointing on his ministry. That young man's name was Billy Graham.

Today I feel a special closeness to Billy Graham. He is one of God's special answers to my praying, as well as others'. I rejoice in the way God has used Billy to touch kings and presidents and millions of others for Him.

Over the years God has kept reworking my set of priorities, and as I have grown older He has led me to spend an increasing number of hours with Him in a ministry of intercession.

Very early in the morning, before the day's distractions begin at Capitol Manor in Salem, Ore., the alarm calls me to prayer. I prepare a food tray the night before so that I am more alert as I talk with the Lord. The hours speed by much too quickly because there is so much to discuss with Him.

Does praying cost anything? Yes. It means refusing invitations because an early morning prayer time begins with early retirement the night before. But I wouldn't miss this fellowship for anything.

What can one find to talk to God about for so many hours? The better you know Him, the more there is to say just about Him—praise, adoration, worship, these become meaningful experiences.

And then there's the whole world! God leads me to pray for rulers and presidents, for stability of governments in troubled places, for people in famine areas, for qualified national leadership, for national pastors and churches. Also for an outpouring of God's Spirit on His people, for our country, our students, our State Department, our congressmen, for our President and his advisors, for local government officials; for missionaries, for literature needs, for orphans, for radio ministries and for my friends.

My prayer concern can be traced back to my youth, when I spent several summers under the influence of men like Dr. A. B. Simpson and the fellowship which grew around his ministry—the Christian and Missionary Alliance. His great biblical expositions on God's character and holiness, and his missionary zeal, contributed profoundly to my life.

At 17, I gave my life to God for missionary

service. I still remember the moment so clearly, standing by our old-fashioned icebox, singing, "I would walk alone with Jesus. . . ." I told Him He would be my treasure and I would go wherever He sent me.

Now, in the sunset of life, I can attest to His great faithfulness—so great, in fact, that He showers His blessings in ways beyond human comprehension. Take the memorable encounter I alluded to earlier.

It was a beautiful Lord's Day morning in late 1974. The church was filled with worshipers who had gathered to sing God's praises and to hear the Word from the Lord and His servant.

After the service I greeted friends and newcomers, then left for the Manor. That is my lovely home in Salem, Oregon.

That day the menu included baked chicken, always a favorite of mine. As I started to eat, suddenly I realized something was wrong—I couldn't handle the knife and fork; my face became distorted, and then the right side of my body became lifeless.

I tried to excuse myself without being noticed. A friend beside me offered to go with me to the Infirmary, which was close by. By then my foot was twisting.

We managed to get to the Infirmary and there I must have collapsed. What transpired, I am not sure, but when I came to consciousness I was in a bed with nurses hovering around. The next two or three days I was more or less oblivious to all around me. My right side and speech had been greatly affected.

About a week later, as I began to think more clearly, the familiar Word of God came to me: "Is anyone sick? He should call for the elders of the church and they should pray over him and pour a little oil upon him, calling on the Lord to heal him. And their prayer, if offered in faith, will heal him, for the Lord will make him well" (James 5:14, 15). It became clear to me: *that is what I must do.*

Three elders of our church, men of faith and prayer, came to the Infirmary at my request. With great joy I greeted them, believing the Lord was going to work even as I had obeyed the Word.

Each one prayed and one anointed me. Then faith began to well up in my heart—faith to believe God had heard and answered. Resurrection life began to flow into my body, with its healing power.

In a few days my voice came back; the hand with which I could only write a few scratches and the twisted foot became normal. My emotions stabilized.

My doctor son advised surgery to clear the clots from the left aorta.

Now, one year later, the whole body is well again, with no handicap in speech or walking.

God has taught me many lessons in this blessed experience. I am again aware how fearfully and wonderfully we are made. Because of this, I realize anew the truth of God's Word: "Haven't you yet learned that your body is the home of the Holy Spirit God gave you, and that he lives within you? Your own body does not belong to you. For God has bought you with a great price. So use every part of your body to give glory back to God, because he owns it" (1 Corinthians 6:19, 20).

Also: "But this precious treasure—this light and power that now shine within us—is held in a perishable container, that is, in our weak bodies. Everyone can see that the glorious power within must be from God and is not our own" (2 Corinthians 4:7).

What a sacred trust is committed to us to maintain these bodies. We should carefully follow that which will maintain them in health—proper food, proper exercise, and proper thinking which comes from meditation on the Word of God.

Not only did God wonderfully heal me, but He also gave me three rewarding areas of witness.

The first and most important is the study of the Word in the early hours of the day, when the world around is bathed in silence and the Presence of the Holy One is so exceedingly precious, leading to worship.

Second, the Word then leads to praise, prayer, intercession—even travail in the Spirit. Adoration of the Lamb is followed naturally—no, supernaturally—by prayer for those in authority, for God's servants on the mission fields, for God's work and servants here in our own land, for personal needs.

Third is the ministry of counseling. From all parts of our land come letters asking for prayer and counsel. Then in our College Camp there is the joy of ministering to teenagers and college young people, especially sharing the deep things of God, cultivating hunger and thirst for the Lord.

My life has been filled with rich blessings, yet these past years have been in some ways the sweetest of them all.

ARMIN R. GESSWEIN was trained and
ordained in the Lutheran ministry, and is a
graduate of Concordia Theological Seminary, St.
Louis, Missouri. He ministered extensively in
Norway's great spiritual revival during 1937 and
1938. He served there among all the leading
evangelical denominations.

Since returning to America, he has ministered widely among the churches of this country, promoting New Testament evangelism. For three years Gesswein was a member of the faculty of Gordon College and Gordon Divinity School in Wenham, Massachusetts.

He is the founder and director of the "Minister's Revival Prayer Fellowship" which took shape first in Los Angeles, California. This is an interdenominational fellowship which, through many city-wide prayer groups of ministers and special revival conferences, aims to help pastors and churches of all Christian groups in New Testament revival and evangelism.

He has been chairman of the Spiritual Life Commission of the National Association of Evangelicals. He was associate evangelist on the Billy Graham team in the New York Crusade, also on the staff of the Greater Los Angeles Billy Graham Crusade, a Crusade Associate on the Billy Graham team and a leader of a plenary session at the Berlin World Congress on Evangelism. He was also a delegate to the World Evangelization Congress in Lausanne, Switzerland.

Not Knowing Whither I Went
Armin R. Gesswein

How God led me from Long Island . . . to
Norway . . . to revival . . . to a wife . . . to the
full plan for my life involves many memorable
encounters with Him. What an exciting
adventure, in this day of "discovery," when
horoscopes are all the rage and ouija boards are
outselling Monopoly.

"You shall receive power, after that the Holy
Spirit is come upon you; and you shall be
witnesses unto Me, both in Jerusalem, and in all
Judea, and in Samaria, and unto *Norway!*" (Of
course, Acts 1:8 says "to the uttermost part of
the earth" . . . and for me that was Norway.) In
Hammerfest a marker reminded me that I was in
the northernmost town of the world—the
uttermost part.

Psalm 37:5 took me to Norway: "Commit your
way unto the Lord, trust also in Him, and He
shall bring it to pass." To find my wife, I had to
back up one verse: "Delight yourself also in the
Lord, and He shall give you the desires of your
heart." And all of this happened in a strange land.

Many people think I am Norwegian. They
know of my association with Norway, and my
having been involved in the great spiritual
awakening there. But I had no connections
whatever in Norway. When God led me to
Norway, He had several surprises in store for me.

First, I knew only one person there, a man
from America, but I had no idea in what part of
Norway he was.

Then, I didn't know the language, except one
word, "ikke"—and I really was not sure what it
meant.

Further, the idea that I was to stay on in
Norway never even entered my mind. I was
pastor of a congregation in Garden City Park,
Long Island, and had told my people I would be
back in about six weeks. On the Sunday when I
said "Good-bye" to my people, some wept.
"We'll never see you here as our pastor any
more," they said. "I'll be back in a few weeks,"
I assured them. But I never got back, and that
was the end of my pastoral ministry. They must
have seen something I didn't.

I had never dreamed of preaching in Norway.
But when it all became clear, I purchased a
third-class ticket on a huge Cunard Lines ship.

That God had a wife waiting for me in
Norway—a wonderful wife, the best girl of all
Norway—had not crossed my mind. Where? Far
up in north Norway, several hundred miles north
of the Arctic Circle. Almost as far as one can go
in this world. If God could find a wife for me
way up there, there is hope for anybody!

This was before the war and there was revival
in Norway. In the night meetings, after the
service seemed over, people went out and
brought others in. Some responded to the
invitation through the hours of the night. How
glad I was to be a part of this exciting scene.

Many ask me how God led me to go. I had
written to a Christian leader in London, asking
some questions about New Testament
Christianity. One day I received a lovely reply,
and his closing paragraph read: "Now I wonder,
would it not be possible for you to come over
for a time of fellowship?"

No, thanks, I thought. I was glad for the letter,

and the other things he wrote. But I had no desire to cross the Atlantic, so I laid the letter aside. But God gave me no rest, and I spread the letter out on my bed before the Lord. Almost as soon as I did so, I knew I was to go to London.

How can I possibly leave, with all that is stacked up now? It seemed so impossible. As I walked, I began to pray: "Lord, if this is of You, do three things: 1) make all the signals green; 2) supply the money for the trip without my saying anything to anyone about finances; 3) supply the right man for my church in my absence." I thought of the Scripture: "Commit everything you do to the Lord. Trust him to help you do it and he will" (Ps. 37:5).

Still walking on, suddenly these words seemed to be circulating through my being: *And you'll go to Norway too!* This kind of an experience I never seek. But it was as real as if the Lord Jesus Christ was right there saying it. Somehow, I thought of Mary, the mother of Jesus. She believed, and did not doubt. *Lord, I believe it,* I quickly said.

Beautiful, indeed, was the way He answered. All the signals began to turn green. A man gave me a check one day to "use as led." The Lord reminded me, "There's your money for the trip."

"What about your church?" I was standing in Times Square one day, talking with a minister friend from another part of the state. We "just happened" to meet there. Later I was reminded to write and ask him to supply for me. He was sorry but would not be able to come. "Lord," I said, "that signal is red." But He reminded me it was not yet time for me to leave. Soon another letter came. My friend would come, if I still wanted him. The last signal had turned green.

I'll never forget that day in March when I left

the New York harbor aboard the old *Berengaria*
(Cunard Lines) on one of its last trips. Newsmen
and photographers were all around, because our
ship—together with the Italian *Rex* and the classy
French liner, the *Normandie*—were all in the
harbor, something which seldom ever happened.

I felt like Abraham, who "went out not
knowing whither he went." First, to England. In
Bristol one day I was very much moved, standing
in John Wesley's stable and viewing the harness
of his famous horse . . . then near-by in his
famous chapel . . . then kneeling where he often
knelt by a famous window with the ledge where
he had his Bible. Then came George Mueller's
famous orphan homes. All this activated my faith
and praying.

The next morning, in devotions, I sensed that
God would have me take the first fast train I
could back to London, and that now He wanted
me to go to Norway. All was bright in London
that day as I came to the guest-house. I asked
whether any mail had come for me. I had been
gone a few weeks, and was concerned for my
congregation. No—but just then the postman
came. One of the top letters was for me—from
Norway!

Before leaving Long Island, I obtained some
sort of address for the only man I knew to be in
Norway from the U.S.—Rev. E. M. Anderson, a
Norwegian evangelist, one of my dearest friends
in America. In Norway he would be moving all
about in meetings, so I simply posted a letter to
him with the prayer that somehow it would reach
him. Well, there was a letter from him, at that
moment! And, would you believe it, from
Bergen, the very city where my boat would
dock! He was in the midst of a strong revival
which moved the whole city, and now he

welcomed me to Norway, and to Bergen.

Crossing the North Sea that week, on the
Venus boat (an overnight trip), I slept little, and
prayed much. *Lord, there is revival in Norway . . .
get me into it as soon as possible—and get it into me.
Don't spare me, whatever the cost.* There I learned
the right way to pray for revival. Such a prayer is
sure to be answered. The very next day God
answered.

When I docked in Bergen, there was my dear
friend. I wanted to pinch myself. "Thank You,
God. You did not lie to me that day on Long
Island when You said, 'And you'll go to Norway
too.' " It was about noon and all through the
hours of that day I knew God was at work all
over the city. I checked in at a hotel where Rev.
Anderson and some of the leaders were staying.
People came through the hours of the afternoon,
convicted of their sins, seeking help and Christ's
forgiveness. (The big word in Norway's revivals
was "Sundenöd" . . . "conviction of sin").

At an early hour in the evening, the streets
thickened with people, all going to "the
meeting." I walked along with my American
friend who would be preaching. He said, "I
want you to give a greeting." "Oh, no," I said,
"there is revival here . . . I have nothing to say
. . . I came to be revived." But he won out, and
I had to sit on the platform. *What a sight,* I said
to myself. *Look at all those people, on an ordinary
weeknight.* They were almost hanging over the
balcony: old folks, young folks, intermingled
throughout.

This was the pattern I was to see in all the
revivals: no gaps—the young and old loving each
other, working together, praying together,
weeping together, sitting together. The old were
young again! As Rev. Anderson was preaching, a

heavenly melting came over the audience,
something like a gentle rain. People began to
weep softly, and pray tenderly. Soon some were
kneeling. More and more knelt, all around, right
where they were. My friend stopped preaching.
The whole large audience, it seemed, turned into
an inquiry room, with people giving their hearts
to Christ right where they were. *Lord, I thank
You. It would have been worth a trip around the
world just for this one meeting.* I knelt in a corner.
*Dear Lord, You are already answering my prayer on
shipboard last night.*

But He was not finished with me. That was
but the beginning. The next week, in Oslo, He
got through all the way to the bottom of my life,
as I was alone some days with my Bible.
Suddenly, in the midst of many tears, He called
me to Norway! The experience was as real as my
conversion.

*I can't . . . I don't know anybody . . don't know
the language . . . haven't a single invitation . . .
don't know one church body from another . . . didn't
come for that . . . have no money . . . and, above all,
I have a congregation back on Long Island. I promised
I would be back. They have many ministers here in
Norway.* But He gave me no peace until I
yielded. He wanted me in Norway.

Soon everything began to happen for me. God
assured me He would take care of everything,
including my congregation. With that call to
Norway my pastoral ministry ended. A brand
new chapter had begun.

Some weeks later, I was preaching in Oslo,
and staying in a Lutheran Mission Hotel. I had
been up in northern Norway, and had heard of
plans being made for a big youth conference,
where Frank Mangs, the noted Swedish
evangelist, was to speak. He was the man God

signally used in the Norway revival, especially in
Oslo. Everyone up north was preparing, and
eagerly awaiting his coming. Also, because the
revival had come mostly to the south of Norway,
they were praying in northern Norway that God
would also send them a visitation.

In that Oslo hotel, I had a real burden for the
northern conference. It was strange. God was
laying messages on my heart and mind. From the
life of Abraham, I made notes. *Why, if anyone
saw you with these notes and thought you had any
idea you were to preach there, they would say you are
crazy!*

I said nothing to anyone. All at once word
came that Mangs could not go . . . he was ill. I
felt bad, for I knew how they were all expecting
him. Then word came the next day that he was
better, and could go. I was glad. Sunday I
preached. No change. Then came Monday
morning, and Rev. Johnson knocked at my door.

"We've been together as a committee," he
said. "Mangs is worse . . . he can't go . . . and
we would like you to go to the youth conference
in his place."

That was the first time anyone ever said
anything to me about my going, *except the Lord.*
Everything in me livened up, and soon I was on
the train to Trondheim, and from there on the
coast boat for Finsnes. It was already Thursday
when I arrived. The conference was moving
along. I knew one man there, a minister from
Trondheim. He was to be my interpreter.

I began at once to give the messages on
Abraham which God had laid on my heart in the
Oslo hotel. They were new to me, and to them.
It pleased the Lord to use them in a rather
remarkable way, and we soon realized He was
giving us a gracious visitation from on high. On

Sunday the building was too small. People came
from all around: by boat, by bicycle, mostly on
foot—some a Norwegian mile or more. (A
Norwegian mile is six or seven of our miles).

The weather was just perfect, so we held the
services outside and used the building for
"after-meetings." I preached from a truck. The
Holy Spirit was at work, beyond expectation. We
prayed with many. All this opened up a big door
for me in Norway. (Later those messages were
printed under the title *Vaag Troens Sprang . . .
Dare Faith's Leap.*)

In that conference—the first of its kind in
northern Norway—was a youth leader from
Tromsö, Reidun Gabrielsen. She had rounded up
others to come and hear Frank Mangs. Instead,
here came a "man from America." In the midst
of all this moving of the Spirit, God had a wife
for me. His ways are perfect, past finding out.
For some years I had committed marriage
entirely to the Lord, and was all taken up with
revival. I had come to the place where I was
willing to "beat the trail alone." That was much
better than to get the wrong one.

What happened? "Be delighted with the Lord.
Then he will give you all your heart's desires"
(Ps. 37:4). Frank Mangs suddenly had
appendicitis. Would you believe it—he lost his
appendix, and I found my wife! Mangs had a
precious experience in the hospital. Not only did
he recover in a hurry, but also out of it came a
new chapter in his own life, including a gift for a
trip to the Holy Land.

Reidun Gabrielsen's life-verse was Matt. 6:6:
"But when you pray, go away by yourself, all
alone, and shut the door behind you and pray to
your Father secretly, and your Father, who
knows your secrets, will reward you." Every day

she would go up to the third floor of their Tromsö home to have a quiet time with her Bible. Among other things, she would pray for a husband, when there "did not seem to be any prospect in town." When we first met she could hardly say "I love you" in English. The next summer we were married, in a little country church up in Malselven valley.

Soon we returned to Long Island, and I began my ministry at large in our land. Sometimes my wife and I share together in a meeting. With young people, I sometimes speak on "How to Find Your Wife" and she will speak on "How to Find Your Husband."

I left New York harbor with a suitcase and a half. Nearly two years later, I returned with a wife and many suitcases. God has been good to us. We have had many new testings, but these have always led to new blessings. We have three children: Dick, Sonja, and Carol. My wife used to say, "They keep us happy, humble, and poor!" Our encounters with God have been most rewarding. We give all praise to Him.

DR. VERNON CARL GROUNDS
was born and educated in New Jersey and was a
Phi Beta Kappa graduate. He received his B.A.
from Rutgers University. His B.D. was granted
by Faith Theological Seminary and his Ph.D. by
Drew University, where he wrote a doctoral
dissertation on "The Concept of Love in the

Psychology of Sigmund Freud." Wheaton College awarded him the Doctor of Divinity degree in 1956.

For ten years he pastored the Gospel Tabernacle in Paterson, New Jersey, during which time he taught at the American Seminary of the Bible, the Hawthorne Evening Bible School, and The King's College. From 1945 to 1951 he was dean and professor of theology at Baptist Bible Seminary in Johnson City, New York. He joined Conservative Baptist Seminary in 1951 as dean, becoming its president five years later.

Dr. Grounds has traveled extensively, preaching in hundreds of churches and lecturing at colleges, universities, and seminaries all across the country. He has served on the faculty of the Young Life Institute, besides participating in both American and Canadian Bible conferences.

Author of *The Reason for Our Hope, Evangelicalism and Social Responsibility, Revolution and the Christian Faith, Emotional Problems and the Gospel,* Dr. Grounds also co-authored the book *Is God Dead?* and has contributed to a number of symposia and encyclopedias. Monthly he writes for *Christian Heritage.*

His major avocation is counseling, to which he devotes as much time as his administrative and teaching responsibilities will allow. He directs the M.A. in Counseling which the Seminary offers.

Aside from membership on the boards of evangelical agencies, Dr. Grounds is the permanent secretary-treasurer of the Evangelical Theological Society.

Coincidence or Providence?
Vernon C. Grounds

Self-deception is by no means uncommon. Ask any counselor, whether Christian or non-religious, about that. We all have an astonishing capability of pulling the wool over our own eyes and performing the wool-pulling trick without being aware that we are doing it.

In the New Testament, therefore, the Holy Spirit warns us: "If any man among you seem to be religious, and bridleth not his tongue, but deceiveth his own heart, this man's religion is vain" (James 1:26).

That warning reminds us of another warning text in the Old Testament: "The heart is deceitful above all things, and desperately wicked: who can know it?" (Jeremiah 17:9). Jeremiah seems to be saying that the human psyche is like a subterranean labyrinth with a maze of twisting tunnels where our minds become dizzy and disoriented.

Thus when we look back on our experience, it is very easy to be victimized by self-deception. How readily memory slips a few cogs! We exaggerate or overdramatize. A simple event is dressed up until the truth can no longer be recognized under the imaginative overlay. And this is especially the case when we are telling about our God-experiences. For by what criteria can we distinguish an encounter with the ultimately Real from some purely psychological reaction?

God is undoubtedly able to verify Himself and

verify Himself unmistakably. Yet the danger of deception persists. There is, then, no safeguard against unintentional distortion and inflation of past happenings except a prayerful, ruthless winnowing of nonfactual chaff from experiential wheat.

What has been my most unmistakable encounter with God? Frankly, I cannot recall any one particular occurrence and assert, "That was it. I experienced God at that point and in that situation as never before nor since." Instead of being able to recall one peak experience, I can recall a cumulative series of experiences which across the years have deepened my trust and commitment. Let me share them as accurately and unsensationally as I can.

My conversion was not a spiritual high. With my childhood faith, such as it was, reduced to near zero by my first year of college reading and study, I returned home for summer vacation and began to fellowship with some of the young people whom I had previously known in high school. They had, allegedly, undergone conversion. So they were spending much of their time in hymn-singing, praying and witnessing.

Thinking that they offered an interesting opportunity for psychological observation, I went one Sunday night to a gathering in a nearby home. As I listened and watched, I realized that something had indisputably occurred in their lives. They were strangely different from what I had known them to be.

How explain the difference? Maybe, I thought to myself, God is for real. Maybe the gospel is true after all. Maybe Jesus Christ is more than a myth; maybe He is a supernatural reality, able to change people. Half skeptically, half seriously, therefore, as members of the group were praying out loud one after the other, I too prayed, asking God, if He was real, to show me that Jesus Christ was His son and could be my Savior.

I had no identifiable reaction whatever except a twinge of amusement at the fervent jubilation of those ardent Christians. Yet at the bottom of my heart I meant that prayer. If God were real, I wanted Him to reveal Himself to me through Jesus Christ. He did. He revealed Himself not especially that night but slowly in the weeks and months which followed as I forced myself to pray, read Scripture, and share with my old/new friends. I cannot honestly report, however, that my initial experience was mysteriously and overwhelmingly divine in nature. Encounter? Well, there was nothing that I felt could be properly so designated.

As I moved on in my Christian life, I did have an experience which brought a strong sense of divine reality. I was driving by myself in the evening, singing rather softly:

> *My sin—O, the bliss of this glorious thought,*
> *My sin—not in part but the whole,*
> *Is nailed to the cross and I bear it no more,*
> *Praise the Lord, praise the Lord, O, my soul!*

Suddenly—and I can still pinpoint the spot though the experience occurred forty years ago—I felt engulfed by God's love, so engulfed that I started to weep. A moving awareness of Presence gripped me. How long it persisted I cannot say—probably a matter of a few minutes. Yet still today—and I am now in my early sixties—I vividly recall my reaction as a man in his early twenties. That tear-inducing sensation like a less-than-low voltage electric current—was it only a psychological reaction? As I interpret the experience, it was a psychological reaction no doubt, but a psychological reaction triggered by an encounter with God.

Some years later I was caught up in a rather ugly situation which threatened to destroy a school at which I had begun to teach only a few months before. Under extraordinary pressure, I kept praying for some reassuring indication of God's guidance. What was I to do, a wholly innocent bystander who had been forced willy-nilly to become a participant in a distressing controversy?

Should I resign or should I stay and struggle to set right things that were in my opinion wretchedly wrong? I distinctly remember the time of day and the very spot on the street where, as I was walking and subvocally praying, confusion abruptly clarified, uncertainty gave way to calm decisiveness and a sense of God's sustaining strength took possession of me.

It would not be truthful to assert that "heaven came down and glory filled my soul." Neither do I think that with integrity I can testify God spoke to me. Yet as I analyze what took place there on that street I must declare that God ministered to me as directly and definitely as if He had spoken audibly. Whatever may have been the psychological factors, my reaction that morning was triggered by a God-encounter.

One summer it was my privilege to teach a course in Christian Apologetics at the Young Life Institute in Colorado. Though the field was thoroughly familiar to me, I simply buried myself in reading and reflection, once again probing in depth the case for unbelief. I grappled afresh with the arguments against supernaturalism advanced by some of the most powerful minds in Western civilization from Democritus down through Nietzsche to Bertrand Russell.

The arguments were hackneyed, but I began to feel their force and cogency as never before. And I gradually grew more and more inwardly disturbed. How answer the skeptical analyses of David Hume and Immanuel Kant? How refute the naturalistic reductionism of Feurerbach and Freud? What adequate explanation is there for the agonizing mystery of evil?

Maybe some of my psychologist-friends were more perceptive than I. Maybe I believed because I was emotionally motivated. Maybe all my lecturing and writing to establish the truth of Christianity was a piece of protracted rationalization. During those days of probing debate, I understood viscerally why some keen-minded and evidently sincere people opt for atheism. But as I studied and pondered, I kept praying.

Every afternoon by myself I walked westward, facing the beauty and majesty of the Rampart Range of the Rocky Mountains outside Colorado Springs. One afternoon as I walked and thought and prayed, I no longer saw the landscape around me. I saw a mindscape. I saw with my imagination, not my reason. I saw a godless universe, an empty desolation worse than a frozen hell. And as I walked and thought and prayed I saw another mindscape.

I saw or I grasped the magnificent meaning, the almost breath-constricting joy, the radiance of a reality pervaded by and centered in Jesus Christ. Anyone observing me would have detected, I suspect, no change in my gait. I kept steadily walking westward, but within I was experiencing an upward soaring of spirit, an exhilarating sense of liberation, the kind of exultation that comes when listening to great music.

God! God! God! Yes, an engulfing, reassuring awareness of God filled my being—not merely my psyche but my whole being. The atheistic arguments were not answered, yet the fierce turmoil of the inner debate ceased. I knew why Job exclaimed, "I have heard of thee with the hearing of the ear, but now mine eye seeth thee." I did not see, yet I saw! My psychologist friends may explain that experience as they like. I explain it as a God-encounter.

One morning before 7:30 I parked my car, as I usually do, directly outside the administrative building where I have my office. Since there is a fairly long driveway leading down to the parking area, I never gave a thought to the possibility that the car might be stolen. So I left it for a student who had agreed to take it for minor repairs. Mid-morning he came to my office asking where it was. With some surprise I told him that I had left it in its usual place. I was even more surprised when he informed me that the car was not there. Thinking the student mistaken, I went to look for myself. He was not mistaken. The car was gone. A prank perhaps? No prank. Theft. I notified the police and my insurance company, then hopefully awaited the car's return.

On Tuesday mornings I was meeting in my office, as I still do, to fellowship and pray with a group of students. Naturally we asked God to have the car returned, and returned undamaged. But after several weeks had passed, my faith began to waver. Thousands of cars are stolen each year and never returned to their owners. I was therefore proceeding to arrange a settlement with my insurance company and start the search for the best second-hand car I could buy with that sadly meager settlement. Yet every Tuesday morning one of the students brought the same request to God's attention: "Lord, please let us see the car back in its parking place outside." And at times his request was, I thought, overly presumptuous: "Father, we want that car back in its parking place." I admired that student's stubborn persistence and insistence though I had given up praying for my car's return.

But after a trip out of town, I was met at the airport by my very happy wife. Our car had been found undamaged, except for the ashtray which we never used. Somebody had left it on a busy street in Colorado Springs. A few days later I stood with that student who had stubbornly kept on praying for the car's return. And there it was back in its usual parking place, undamaged. Coincidence or providence?

I had been preparing an address for a conference that would bring together evangelical leaders from many missionary agencies and fields as well as from churches and schools to consider more effective strategies of witness to Roman Catholics. One of the books I used was an out-of-print volume. I happened, I thought, to own a copy of it.

As I was writing the final draft, I discovered that the book had disappeared. That meant I could not include some essential information in my bibliography. I hunted everywhere in my library at our Seminary and at home. (Years ago when the number passed 10,000, I stopped counting the books I own. Since I am a bibliophile, they are all over any place I occupy!)

Our seminary library staff, my secretary, and I tried everywhere to borrow another copy of that book. None was obtainable. Finally the day came when my manuscript had to be mailed for printing. The book was still missing. I ransacked my shelves and stacks once again without success.

I made some long-distance telephone calls. No success.

I sat at my desk and told the Lord that, while it was a rather trifling matter, I absolutely needed that reference within a few hours. I had already repeatedly asked Him to help me locate my copy of the book. Now I specifically asked Him to help me find it by early afternoon. That seemed impossible, but I made the request anyway.

I had scheduled lunch with a student. He volunteered to drive. But his car refused to start. So we walked back to my car. I unlocked the door on the driver's side, got in and, reaching over the seat, released the lock on the opposite side. The right-hand door of that very aged car (bought, as I remember, for $500!) was almost never opened. I drove the car alone back and forth to my office and around town; and since I was almost always its sole occupant, the right-side door stayed unopened months on end. But that noon I opened it. Something fell out at the feet of my student-guest. It was the missing book. Somehow long weeks previously it had slipped down between the seat and the next-to-never-opened door. No wonder I could not find it! After lunch, though, I sat down and with thanks to God completed my bibliography. Coincidence or providence?

One additional experience I regard as an indubitable instance of God's intervention. I had been trying to help a friend whose battle against emotional deterioration was slowly turning into a defeat. Her psychiatrist, who had little sympathy with her Christian convictions, put her in the closed ward of a local hospital. Steadily her condition grew worse.

Afraid of vegetating in a state institution, my friend became acutely distressed. Since her

husband was dead, the psychiatrist in charge
notified other members of her immediate family to attend a hearing at which a group of doctors and officials could reach a decision regarding her commitment to the state institution she so dreaded. The hearing was held; a decision to commit was reached.

The day before she was scheduled to be taken to the place which, rightly or wrongly, she so dreaded, I visited my friend. She was allowed to leave the locked ward in my care, and so we spent some time talking and praying. As our visit ended and we stood together, she inside the threshold, I outside her ward, I was prompted to say, "If God wants to unlock this door and have you walk out free, He can do it." That was still my eleventh hour prayer.

Early the next morning my friend's psychiatrist, rather nonplussed, telephoned me. He could not quite account for what he was going to do. He had decided to reverse the commitment decision. He had decided not to place my friend in the state institution. Instead he would release her into my custody if I was willing personally to be responsible for her.

With no hesitancy I assented. It was my thrill, consequently, to walk into that local hospital a little later and stand outside the door until it was unlocked from within by an attendant. And my friend walked through it into freedom and into a future of emotional health, fruitful Christian witness, and rare happiness with a new husband. A concatenation of circumstances? No, God's intervention! I believe He unlocked that door and set my friend free.

As I think back across the years of my life, I recall experiences which I can explain to my own satisfaction only by reference to God's

intervention. Yet I realize, as I have been
mentioning, that some of my non-Christian
friends are skeptical about God's very existence
and therefore they explain my experiences
naturalistically rather than supernaturalistically.
They admit that I have undergone certain
experiences, but they argue that God had
nothing to do with those experiences—because,
quite simply, there is no God. Let me, then, put
the issue squarely. Two explanations of my
experiences are possible: God or no God. And I,
as the experient, opt unequivocally for the
God-explanation.

DR. CARL F. H. HENRY is
lecturer-at-large for World Vision, International,
and has flown almost a million miles by air,
lecturing and preaching on every continent of
the world.

He is the founding editor and now
editor-at-large of *Christianity Today* magazine. Dr.

Henry was the chairman of the 1970 Jerusalem Conference on Biblical Prophecy.

In addition he has authored twenty books as well as editing others including: *Contemporary Evangelical Thought Series* (5 volumes), and *Baker's Dictionary of Christian Ethics.*

Dr. Henry is listed in *Who's Who in the World, Who's Who in Religion, The Dictionary of International Biography,* and *Men of Achievement.*

He is the former vice-president of the American Theological Society, and former president of the Evangelical Theological Society.

God's Express to St. George's
Carl F. H. Henry

As the crow flies it is less than five kilometers
(about three miles) from Montreaux to Clarens,
Switzerland. By daylight this countryside brims
with charm, but at night it sometimes vanishes
under an inky fog that only God can probe and
overwhelm. I remember one such dismal night
when at wit's end I battled that lonesome road
and prayed for divine help.

It was late in July, 1953.

After a dozen years of graduate teaching on
several campuses I had finally gotten my first
sabbatical—a fall term from Fuller Seminary
where the 1947 founding faculty had invested,
and gladly, immeasurable energies. Despite what
was then considered an exceptional salary among
evangelicals ($8500) my financial resources were
strained by the completion of doctoral studies,
accumulating a good working library of several
thousand theological books, and meeting
mortgage payments on our Pasadena home.

My sights were set on Scotland—more
particularly on New College, Edinburgh—for an
unhurried spate of research and study. The
children (then eleven and nine), my wife, Helga,
and her widowed mother who lived with us,
planned to remain at home. Even so, the cost of
just transatlantic travel would bite deeply into our
meager reserves. The Fulbright scholarship for
which I had applied was sabotaged, I learned, by a
professor who considered my evangelical views too
unrepresentative of the American religious scene.

Then I heard about a three-day conference in Switzerland (July 28–30, 1953) scheduled by World Evangelical Fellowship, that also included a New York-to-Geneva charter flight. When days before departure time a family emergency forced one of the delegates to cancel out I was invited to participate as an observer. I was on my way to Edinburgh, a bit circuitously, to be sure, but definitely on the way and for less than $100.

The word "circuitously," may I say, has hidden meanings, for the very night of arrival in Geneva triggered an unforgettable experience— one that involved, incredible as it seems, meeting God's messenger on a motorcycle. There were wheels in Ezekiel's vision, and the Old Testament also says something about Jehu's furious driving. Unlike them I had neither a prophetic revelation nor a miraculous manifestation, but when it comes to a providential answer to prayer no one can gainsay me.

The W.E.F. conference was to convene at St. George's School in Clarens, a village near Montreaux on the shores of Lake Geneva. I had determined to make my sabbatical yield literally daily rewards in theological learning, so, sending my luggage ahead to Clarens on the charter flight's special motorcoach, I stayed behind in Geneva for an evening's theological conversation.

I had prearranged to meet Walter Marshall Horton, an influential liberal Protestant theologian who, somewhat under the same Barthian influences that impinged on Reinhold Niebuhr, had switched to a more "realistic" view of human nature and had accordingly somewhat adjusted his former view of sin and redemption. We walked the misty shores of Lake Geneva for more than two hours that night, conversing about biblical and contemporary theology and particularly about the issues of general and special revelation.

Inevitably the time came when I had to hasten to the railway station for the last train to Montreaux and then—as W.E.F. correspondence had led me to believe—for a short taxi junket or perhaps even a brisk walk to the conference center. When the train made its sudden and brief stop at Montreaux, only a Swiss lass of about twenty and I got off. Sensing that I was a stranger, she understandably hurried away. The station was locked, there were no cabs, and no one was in sight.

In a fearsome French that must have frightened even the nestled birds I called out "Madamoiselle! Madamoiselle!" It was more than I dared hope but the young lady actually reappeared. I flashed before her a note with the words: CLARENS—ST. GEORGE'S SCHOOL. Nodding knowingly she indicated nearby streetcar tracks and signaled the direction I should take. I pointed to my wrist watch, going through a charade that dramatized the possible soon arrival of a tram. Just as dramatically she vehemently shook her head and pointed to the midnight sky. Public transportation had turned in for the night. Again motioning to me to follow the car tracks, she vanished once more into the night.

The weather was damp; in fact, a light rain was falling. But I set out, walking on and on—expecting at each turn to see the anticipated Clarens. But there was only the dark lake, and a penetrating cold wind that whipped the worsening rain about me. I turned up my coat collar, pulled down my hat to ward off the migraine to which I was easily susceptible.

Slogging on, I came upon a small village, but if there was any identifying signpost I never saw it. Not a shop was open, not a soul was abroad, not a light gleamed from any window.

I was exhausted. I had flown from Los Angeles to New York and thence to Geneva in the piston-type planes then in use, and had spent a full evening in theological dialogue. Counting various time zones, I was in my second full day without sleep. My clothes were damp and I felt chilled. My back, my legs, every muscle ached. So I stretched out on a bench located at what in daytime probably was a tram stop, and used my V.I.P. case as a pillow. But I turned uncomfortably from side to side and, fearing that I might take cold in the raw wet weather, finally started on my way again.

In the distance I finally saw a reflection of lights that might be a police headquarters or fire station. It was, in fact, a large open barn where several coveralled workers were washing down nocturnally-retired street cars for their next morning's operation. I interrupted their hosing activities long enough to show my card: CLARENS—ST. GEORGE'S SCHOOL. The men waved their hands and arms energetically in the direction toward which I had been traveling; the possibility that Clarens was still far distant added to my dismay. I pointed once again to the car tracks as well as in the direction they had indicated and received the unmistakable communication: follow the tracks and eventually you'll get there. Off I went.

Before long I glimpsed a lighted mansion on a distant hill. Believing my exhausting walk was near its end, I started up the dimly-outlined driveway toward the house. I had hardly taken fifty steps when two or three furiously barking monsters came tearing down the hill. Fortunately we were separated by what I had not noticed before—a tall iron mesh fence and a firmly locked gate. There was no gatekeeper or watchman, so this obviously was only a private residence. Somewhat crestfallen, I stumbled back to the street car tracks.

Every two or three blocks I stopped to rest. It was now almost three in the morning, and the rain still gushed in fits and starts. There was occasional lightning. I was bone weary, but I did not want to sleep lest I be pounced upon by thieves. While they might not discover my money-belt, they might take off with my wallet that contained part of my precious Edinburgh survival funds.

After the first of those wearying miles I had begun singing some of the old hymns; after the second I resorted to more vigorous modern gospel songs. It was like shifting from regular to "extra" gasoline (I deliberately do not say premium or high test!) But by now I had stopped singing—even on the same note, as I'm prone to do. Instead I breathed a prayer from time to time. I was at the fag end of strength.

Mentally I recalled the day of my conversion to Christ, then my response to His vocational call, the gracious and multiple promises of God, and the many blessings and answered prayers I had experienced.

"Please get me to Clarens," I pleaded—not once, but again and again—as I walked and rested and walked and rested.

All at once through the dark, soggy night came a peculiar roar like that of a small truck or an auto with muffler trouble. Soon a feeble light flickered through the rain and gradually brought into view a motorcycle. I determined to flag down the rider, but he was already slowing to a halt. I quickly fumbled for my CLARENS memo but even before I found it he pointed to the rear rack and beckoned me to get on board.

I had never in my life been on a motorcycle,

front or rear, and this challenge was formidable
to say the least. Years before, surgeons had
uncovered a hip mobility problem that explained
why even riding a bicycle was a devastating
experience, not to mention riding a camel in
Egypt. But I climbed on side-saddle, gripping the
driver's belt with one hand and my V.I.P. case
with the other. From the moment my angel took
off—I knew not where—I was terrified; he
accelerated the vehicle unevenly, swerved
unpredictably; at last, with a sudden shout he
swung off into an ascending driveway and
deposited me at the doorstep of St. George's
School.

In my lifetime I have shared magnificent
Cadillacs and Jaguars; I have sailed on luxury
yachts; I have flown in private planes. But in my
long span of memories I classify none of these as
God's Chariot. That designation is reserved alone
for the raucous motorcycle that propelled me
over those remaining miles to Clarens and St.
George's School.

The driver spoke no English and refused my
offer of money. I do not know whether he was a
car barn worker on his way home or a villager
who had stopped there and had learned about
my predicament. All I am sure of is that God
answered my prayer.

At St. George's School the desk clerk had
retired at midnight and would not resume his
work until 6 A.M. That gave me two hours to
stretch out in the reception room. I built a bed of
sofa cushions on the floor, took off my wet shoes
and coat, and literally dropped to sleep. I knew
that God had dispatched an angel on a motorcycle,
and that His special providence in Switzerland
that night was only the remarkable prelude to an
even more rewarding sabbatical in Scotland.

DR. DAVID M. HOWARD is missions
director of Inter-Varsity Christian Fellowship. He
coordinates the total missions emphasis of
Inter-Varsity on college campuses. He was
director of the Tenth Inter-Varsity Missionary
Convention—Urbana 73—held at Urbana,
Illinois, in December 1973, attended by over

14,000 delegates. He also served as director of
the 1976 URBANA Convention.

Dr. Howard served for fifteen years
(1953–1968) with the Latin America Mission in
Colombia and Costa Rica where he was assistant
general director. He now serves on the Board of
Trustees of the Latin America Mission. He is also
on the Board of Directors of the
Interdenominational Foreign Mission Association
and the Wheaton College Board of Trustees.

Dr. Howard holds a B.A. in Liberal Arts and
an M.A. in Theology, both from Wheaton
College (Illinois). In May of 1974 he received
the honorary degree, Doctor of Laws (LL.D.)
from Geneva College, Beaver Falls,
Pennsylvania. His name appears in *Who's Who,
Men of Achievement,* and *Contemporary Authors.*

As well as writing numerous articles on
missions, he has also written several books:
Words of Fire; Rivers of Tears, a study of the life of
the prophet Jeremiah (Tyndale House, 1976); *By
the Power of the Holy Spirit,* dealing with the place
of the Holy Spirit in missions (InterVarsity Press,
1973); *How Come, God?,* dealing with questions
raised in the book of Job about knowing God in
a personal and living way (A. J. Holman
Company, 1972); *Student Power in World
Evangelism,* on the Biblical, historical, and
contemporary perspectives of missions
(InterVarsity Press, 1970); and *The Costly Harvest,*
on the maturing of the young church in
Northern Colombia (Tyndale House, 1975,
formerly entitled *Hammered As Gold*).

En Route to Completion
David M. Howard

One of my more memorable encounters with God began with an incident which I cannot remember. The only reason I know it happened is that the other person involved remembers it clearly and told it to me years afterwards. The total encounter extends over some years and is not yet completed.

It was a hot and humid afternoon, typical of most days in the historic port city of Cartagena on the Caribbean coast of Colombia. I was driving into the city, returning home from an outlying rural area where I often visited in the course of missionary work. On the outskirts of Cartagena a stranger waved me down, asking for a ride into the center of the city. He was too poor to pay the twenty *centavos* bus fare, which was the equivalent of about two cents in gold currency. So I picked him up, and we conversed during the fifteen-minute drive into the center.

Spontaneous witnessing has never been easy for me and I have more often than not failed in attempting it. But that day I was apparently able to share a brief witness with this stranger, asking about his relationship to God and encouraging him to receive Jesus Christ. Agustin Ramos (for that was his name) told me some years later that that was the first time he had ever heard the gospel.

Agustin worked as a jeweler, renting a stall in the city market where he repaired watches. His income was hardly adequate for his family of eleven children, yet he squandered most of it on liquor and women. He was consorting with fourteen women simultaneously but was not married to any of them. One served as his *companera,* roughly equivalent to a common-law wife, raising the eleven children, but thirteen other women enjoyed his companionship as mistresses of one sort or another. On Sundays he would usually get thoroughly inebriated and spend the day in carousing and fighting, which was very much a pattern of life for the men of his neighborhood.

Agustin finally reached the end of his rope. The Monday morning hangovers were getting too heavy. The pitiful looks of his hungry children were eating into his heart. The deep sorrowful eyes of Margot, his common-law wife who tried hard to raise the family on the pennies left over after his drinking binges, were piercing into his soul. Whatever formal religion he had known previously had proved to be an empty sham. He had tried to work his way out and earn some sort of salvation, only to find such religious efforts to be totally impotent. As a jeweler he had made medallions to be worn around the neck, but he knew perfectly well that these were the work of his hands and not capable of providing salvation.

One Sunday evening, about two years after our "chance" encounter, in desperation he told Margot, "I am going out of this house and I won't return until I find the salvation of my soul." He started down the streets of Cartagena, knowing only that he was looking for deliverance but not having the foggiest idea where or how to find it. The words spoken to him two years previously in the car apparently gave him some clue, but the darkness was very deep.

After wandering for a couple of miles he passed a small evangelical church with the sign "Iglesia del Buen Pastor" (Church of the Good Shepherd). He looked in the open door and noticed a "gringo" preaching. So he slipped in and sat down in the back pew.

At this point my memory begins. I recall seeing a small emaciated-looking man come into church while I was preaching. At the end of the sermon he came unsteadily up the aisle to speak to me. It was rather common in that city for men under the influence of liquor to stagger into a church and sometimes even to engage believers in spiritual talk. But all too often such talk was controlled by their drunken state and was a waste of time. As Agustin approached me I thought, *Here we go again!* His first words to me were, "I have come here looking for the salvation of my soul." His phraseology was almost too evangelical to be real, so I was by now doubly suspicious, wondering if he really knew what he was talking about.

Nevertheless, I decided to give him the benefit of the doubt. We sat down and I explained in simple terms the basic truths of the gospel. In a matter of moments he expressed his desire to receive Jesus Christ as Saviour. We prayed together, but my skepticism remained strong. I was not at all sure that he really understood in his clouded mind what he was doing. If his conversion proved real it would have to be a true miracle of the Holy Spirit.

Shortly after this my family and I returned to the United States on furlough. Therefore, I was unable to do much follow-up work with Agustin. I had no idea of how he was doing spiritually, but I did pray for him and hoped for the best.

Upon returning from furlough I was reminded

with overwhelming force of Paul's words, "And I am sure that God who began the good work within you will keep right on helping you grow in his grace until his task within you is finally finished on that day when Jesus Christ returns" (Phil 1:6). There was Agustin in the church, growing and rejoicing in the Lord. Margot had been so impressed with the sudden and dramatic change in his life that she had given herself to Christ. Together they were now establishing a Christian home and bringing up their children to know the Lord. Agustin had led his mother to the Lord and was working on his father, who also came to Christ in due time.

This was so clearly a work of the Holy Spirit that no man could possibly claim the credit. I had been skeptical on the night Agustin received Christ. I had been unavailable to give him much spiritual nurture immediately thereafter, and no one else had done much aggressive discipling of him. On his own initiative he had broken off relationships with thirteen of his fourteen mistresses, even though some of them did their best to tempt him back into sin. He now remained faithfully with Margot.

After a long process of legal red tape he was able to straighten out his personal relationships and secure a proper marriage license. It was my privilege to perform the wedding of Agustin and Margot in the Buen Pastor Church as a whole bevy of their children looked on in delight. Following their wedding I also had the joy at their request of baptizing them and then standing by as the Colombian pastor received them into formal membership of the church. My wife, Phyllis, befriended Margot in a special way and was instrumental in her growth and encouragement.

But there was still much work for the Holy Spirit to do in bringing to completion the work which He had begun. The Ramos family was tested repeatedly with trials and sorrows which stretched their faith to the limit.

One Saturday morning my wife was driving our jeep into the center of Cartagena to go shopping. Within a few blocks of the main market, where Agustin kept his little jeweler's stall, she saw a tremendous explosion in the market. Billows of black smoke and tons of debris erupted hundreds of feet into the air. A cache of dynamite, illegally being peddled to fishermen, had been set off by a faulty electrical current. The entire center of the market was gutted. Over fifty people were killed and more than nine hundred wounded. Agustin's stall was very close to the center of the explosion.

Total confusion reigned in the city. Ambulances and fire trucks sped to the scene. Rescue efforts went on for hours and even days as debris was cleared, bodies were uncovered, and wounded were rushed to the hospitals amidst the scream of sirens and the wails of grief-stricken friends and relatives of the victims.

Immediately I began to search for Agustin, having determined that he had been at his stall when the explosion occurred. After a search up and down hospital corridors, where wounded were laid out on every available space, I finally located him in an intensive care ward, so badly disfigured and bandaged that I could not recognize him. But the name tag on the bed indicated that it was he. As I stood by his side a doctor approached. I looked up and saw that it was Cartagena's leading bone specialist, an outstanding physician who could provide him with the best care available in Colombia. Since we had known each other previously, we conversed briefly, and he gave me every encouragement that Agustin would recover. It was a miracle that Agustin had even survived, since he had been so close to the center of the explosion where dozens of others had died. It was also a special comfort to see that God had provided him with Cartagena's finest bone specialist and thus the best care available.

God, who had begun His good work in Agustin, had not yet brought it to completion. So He spared his life for a further ministry. Agustin recovered slowly and after many months was able to return to work when the central market was finally reconstructed.

Then God chose to bring further suffering into the family as part of His perfecting process. Their little daughter Yomaira, age three, was stricken with polio. It appeared she would never walk again. They did not have the means to pay for any sort of therapy and only the most limited types of medication. We did what we could to help, but efforts seemed hopeless.

Then one day the S. S. *Hope,* the hospital ship of mercy, sponsored by citizens of the United States concerned for the welfare of developing countries, steamed into the port of Cartagena, and hope revived for the Ramos family. Phyllis and our oldest son, David, Jr., age fifteen, both volunteered to work on board as interpreters for the English-speaking doctors and nurses who could not communicate in Spanish with the Colombian patients.

Through these contacts arrangements were made for Yomaira Ramos to receive the finest kind of therapy known to medical science today. Braces were provided, therapy was given, and within two years Yomaira was once again walking. After we had left Colombia I returned for a visit to Cartagena and, of course, went to the Ramos home among others. As I stepped up to the door of their little cinder block house, one of the first of many children to rush out the door into my arms was Yomaira. What a joy to see the perfecting grace of God at work both physically and spiritually in that family.

In response to God's mercy Agustin felt led to give his life more fully to the ministry. Although he was a faithful witness in leading others to Christ, he desired to give full time to such work. Through the ministry of a local church he was called to become its pastor. Although he lacked formal education for the pastorate, he was willing to work and study, and he soon became an effective leader.

After we left Colombia I stayed in contact with Agustin by mail and rejoiced as God used him to start two new churches in Cartagena. Then I discovered that he had moved to the city of Sincelejo to start another church. Before I could contact him there he had moved to Barranquilla. He had been so successful in establishing the church in Sincelejo that he was able to leave it on its own feet more quickly than expected, and was now planting a new church in Barranquilla. Thus, God, who had begun the good work in him, was continuing to bring it to completion in using him in the lives of many others. He has now established four churches and is working on a fifth.

One day I received a letter from colleagues in Colombia bringing me up-to-date on recent developments. Our mission (the Latin America Mission) had completely reorganized itself and turned total control of all ministries over to national leadership. This means that all

missionaries are now serving under Latin
leadership. They are responsible to Colombian
boards of directors and to Colombian leaders. A
Colombian had been named as executive director
of the entire field of work, a position somewhat
parallel to what I had held as Field Director of
the Latin America Mission. His name was Ramon
Cardona. My heart skipped a beat when I read
this, for I realized the spiritual genealogy that
had taken place.

Several years earlier Agustin had led his
business partner, Roberto, to Christ. Roberto had
led his wife to the Lord. His wife had led her
sister to Christ, who, in turn, had led her
husband, Ramon, to Christ. Thus, Ramon was a
fifth spiritual generation from Agustin, and was
now directing the entire work in the area.

Once again I could only realize that the One
who had begun the good work in the life of
Agustin was continuing to bring it to completion.

But God's work of perfecting will go on until
the day of Jesus Christ. And God's way seems to
be continually to take Agustin and his family
through the depths of suffering. As I write this
chapter I have recently received a letter from him
telling of the kidnapping of his lovely teenage
daughter. For four months they had no clue as to
her whereabouts, but had recently received
information that she was in Venezuela and under
complete control of her kidnappers. The purpose
of the kidnapping could not possibly be for
ransom, as anyone who knows the Ramoses
knows that they barely live from hand to mouth.
Speculation could lead to even more terrifying
reasons such as white slavery. Needless to say, we
are taking what steps we can from this distance
to help Agustin find and recover his daughter.
But only God knows what the result will be.

Thus, this most memorable encounter with God begins with an incident I cannot remember and will end with an ending I cannot predict. The One who is Alpha and Omega only knows the end from the beginning. But it has been exciting to hold on to the truth of God's Word, knowing that "the One who started the good work in (Agustin) will bring it to completion by the day of Jesus Christ."

David M. Howard
page 97

DR. TORREY JOHNSON has been
president and senior minister of the Bibletown
Community Church in Boca Raton, Florida, since
February 11, 1967. In addition to the regular
church activities, Bibletown holds Bible
conferences and concerts, now the largest held
on the North American continent.

Founder of Youth for Christ International, Dr. Johnson has spoken to audiences in Hollywood Bowl; Chicago Stadium; Kiel Auditorium, St. Louis; Maple Leaf Garden, Toronto; Olympia Stadium, Detroit; Boxing Arena, Liverpool, England; and many other leading auditoriums and stadiums throughout the world.

Dr. Johnson has a Bachelor of Science degree from Wheaton College, a Bachelor of Divinity degree from Northern Baptist Theological Seminary, and he has completed all his class work and language requirements for the Th.D. degree from Northern Baptist.

For four years, Dr. Johnson was instructor of New Testament Greek as well as instructor in World History at the Northern Baptist Seminary. He has done post-graduate work at Northwestern University and the University of Chicago.

Dr. Johnson received the following honorary degrees: D.D., Wheaton College, 1945; Hum.D., Bob Jones University, 1945; LL.D., Northwestern College, 1948. He was pastor of the Midwest Church, Chicago for twenty years, 1933–1953.

Dr. Torrey Johnson has conducted large-scale campaigns in many parts of the world including Hong Kong; Vietnam; Bedford, Exeter, England; Swansea, Wales; Jerusalem, Jordan; Oslo, Norway; and Taegu, Korea.

God Does Much More
Torrey M. Johnson

Seated at his desk immediately before me was
the president of the Club Aluminum Corporation
of America, Herbert J. Taylor. He was a
member of the executive board of Chicagoland
Youth for Christ. I had come to him with a
question that desperately needed a solid answer.

"Mr. Taylor, we are having a giant rally in
Soldier Field on Memorial Day, May 30," I
began. "The meeting will cost about $22,000.00.
There is no cover for the stadium which seats
about 100,000 people and if it rains and no
people come to the rally, we will lose
$22,000.00. I haven't got that kind of money.
What do you suggest I do?"

Taylor hesitated a few moments and then
looked up at me with a warm sparkle in his eye.

"Torrey," he said, "did you ever hear about a
man named Elijah who prayed about the
weather? What did God do for him?"

I got the message. I took my hat in my hand,
and turned on my heel. "Thank you, Mr.
Taylor," I said. "You've given me the answer
that I need."

How well did I remember that Elijah prayed
and it rained not upon the earth for three years
and six months, and he prayed again and the
rains came. I knew that I had to pray and ask
God to hold the rains back for just a twenty-four
hour period of time.

We had rented Soldier Field for Memorial Day
with the expectation that people would come to

this first Anniversary Rally of Chicagoland Youth for Christ. They would come from Michigan, Indiana, Wisconsin, Illinois, and some from more distant places. For a period of a month or more, teams of young men and young women had visited towns large and small in the whole area, witnessing in Youth for Christ rallies, working in churches, winning souls, and inviting folk to the rally on this day. Memorial Day would be a focal point. Yes, not only for the midwest, but all America came to look toward Chicago. What would happen on Memorial Day? What a disaster it would be if there was rain. What a victory it could be if God would pour out spiritual blessing!

For the day itself, preparation had been made in the training of a 5,000-voice choir under the direction of T. J. Bittikofer. There was a band of 500 instruments led by Elmer Witthoff. In addition, 500 nurses in uniform were to march down the playing field to form a human cross. Forty marimbas, a number of grand pianos, and electric organs would add to the musical program. What a disaster if rain came and the marimbas were damaged, the brass band could not play, the choir of 5,000 could not sing, and an expected attendance of 75,000 did not materialize.

Laughingly I said to my colleagues and others, "If rain comes and the meeting is not held, I'll go to jail. Working off $22,000.00 at the rate of $1.50 a day, I'll be there for a long time. You've got to help me and you've got to pray."

To discourage us, the weatherman by radio and other media announced there was an unusually rainy season all the month of May. It would continue to rain all day—Memorial Day—in Chicago. We had also the burden of a heavy financial obligation, the expectations of thousands

we hoped would come and the aspirations of
millions who would receive inspiration and
blessing from a great victory. All the ingredients
challenged us to pray, and that we did.

Christians organized prayer meetings
throughout the Chicago area for a number of
days prior to the rally. Small and large groups
met in churches and in homes. On May 29,
scores of leaders met in the second floor Triangle
Restaurant on West Randolph Street in
downtown Chicago. No one needed to be
encouraged to pray. Rain pelted noisily against
the plateglass windows. The rain seemed to mock
our prayers, and it certainly challenged our faith.
Outwardly everything looked hopeless on that
night before the rally. What do you do? You
have to pray . . . pray . . . pray.

Bob Cook, now president of The King's
College, but then the song leader for the
occasion, was there. Billy Graham, who was
going to represent American youth on the
program, was there. Bob Evans, a chaplain in the
United States Navy sent to us to promote the
sale of War Bonds, was there. Many other
Christian leaders, pastors, evangelists, Youth for
Christ men gathered in that second floor
restaurant, and we prayed.

We reminded God how He answered the
prayer of Elijah; how He liberated Peter from
prison; how He stopped the mouths of the lions
for Daniel; how Abraham prayed for the cities of
the plain. Yes, we reminded God of other days
of great miracles and we challenged Him to
answer our prayers now.

Not only was a financial disaster imminent if
He did not answer our prayers, but we felt His
honor and glory were at stake as well. People
knew we were praying. They wondered if God

would meet the need of these people in the midst of all the adverse conditions.

How well we remember those prayers. Some prayed softly, sobbing. Some prayed orderly and properly; others with great concern. One of these was Peter Deyneka, founder of the Slavic Gospel Association. In full voice, he prayed as he looked out the window where the rain pelted down. "O God," he cried out, "you stopped the rain for Elijah; now you must stop the rain for these young people today. Lord, the churches are looking toward us. The world is mocking us. The crowds will be coming. Souls are at stake. Your glory is involved. Lord, be pleased to hear and answer prayer according to your Word."

Amens sounded and resounded all over the room. Fervently and with deep concern Peter prayed on and on. Others preceded him, others followed him. Not until late that night did the prayer meeting come to a close.

Someone asked Deyneka, "When you pray so loud, is it because you don't think God hears?" "No," he laughed, "I know that God hears. Don't worry when I pray loud; God isn't nervous either!"

We spent that night at the Conrad Hilton Hotel on South Michigan in Chicago. We could look out and see Soldier Field in the distance, but more than that we looked beyond toward the eastern shore of Lake Michigan, then on to the sunrise. How shall I explain what happened? It was the morning of Memorial Day. After a rainy night—the climax of a rainy month—the sun came up bright and clear over the city of Chicago. We fell to our knees. Tears stained our cheeks. We lifted our voices to God, "Thank You, Lord, for hearing our prayer; thank You, Lord, for heeding our cry; thank You, Lord, for responding to our need; thank You for the physical token of a spiritual victory this very day."

We arose from our knees and headed for Soldier Field. We saw Chester Scholl, Sr., head usher, driving around on his little electric cart, getting everything in order for what promised to be the biggest gathering of Christians in America in decades. People had said the day of mass evangelism was over; the coming of the Lord was very near. In the last days you must pick them like precious fruit, one by one. Now God was doing a new thing: He was bringing back mass evangelism once again.

As Scholl prepared his ushers, musicians placed their instruments on the stage: 500 brass instruments, 40 marimbas, concert grand pianos and organs. Then came the rehearsal of the band, and the choir, then both together. All morning and all afternoon some six or seven thousand involved themselves in preparation for the big event. Counselors, hundreds of them, gathered to pray and prepare.

All that day the sun shone brightly. Not a cloud appeared overhead. The air stayed warm and fresh, with all the fragrance of burgeoning Spring . . . bursting with leaves and flowers. Amy Anderson followed me everywhere, her notebook in hand. Taking notes, giving instructions, picking up the loose ends and tying things together, she played a vital role in preparation.

As the afternoon wore on and the sun began to sink toward the west, the question arose in our minds again and again, "Will the people come?" No one really knew. More than 20,000 people had jammed the Chicago Stadium on October 22, 1944, but this was May 30, 1945, and Soldier Field could hold up to 100,000 people. Would they come?

We waited. Then the cars began to come down the arteries from the north . . . from the south . . . from the west. From the south came people from Indiana and Michigan and the southern part of Illinois. From the west came people from Western Illinois and Iowa. From the north came others from Minnesota, Wisconsin, and the Dakotas.

The cars kept coming. Traffic jammed the highways. Parking lots quickly filled up. The stadium began to fill. Then suddenly came time for the rally to begin. After the preliminary announcements, Bob Cook led in song, with Doug Fisher at the organ and Merrill Dunlop at the piano. Others assisted at various instruments. Now the stadium had almost reached its capacity. The largest gathering of evangelical Christians and their friends on the North American continent for many years had assembled.

God in His wise providence had provided a wonderful staging for this first anniversary rally of Youth for Christ in Chicago. The week following Memorial Day, the Roman Catholic Archdiocese of Chicago was to host an International Eucharist Congress in Soldier Field. They had to construct all their platforms prior to Memorial Day in order to be ready for their Congress. Because of this, they granted us permission to use their platform for our program. This saved many thousands of dollars and gave us a most attractive setting for the rally. It was wonderful to stand on that platform, provided by our neighbors, and use it to proclaim the Gospel of the Grace of God. Certainly many of our Roman Catholic friends must have been in attendance that day and witnessed this presentation of the gospel. For the added advantage of this facility, we praised God then and we continue to be grateful now.

On the program of the evening, Gil Dodds, at that time the world's record holder for the indoor mile, ran an exhibition race around the track. Then he gave testimony of his faith in Jesus Christ. Others testified. The musicians, including George Beverly Shea, America's beloved baritone, ministered in song. Then the late beloved Percy Crawford delivered the message of the evening. At that time he was director of the Young People's Church of the Air, Philadelphia. Lt. Commander Robert P. Evans gave testimony and also promoted the sale of War Bonds—one of the largest such sales in the history of World War II.

Following the main message, an invitation was given. People streamed out of the stadium stands and onto the playing field. They made public confession of Jesus Christ as Saviour and Lord. Finally it was all over—the message . . . the invitation . . . the benediction.

The rain began to descend softly.

God had answered prayer. No rain fell in Chicago the entire day nor for the entire meeting. To the north of Chicago, to the west, to the south and east, rain descended on Memorial Day. God had put an umbrella over Soldier Field . . . over this great rally of Youth for Christ. "I am going to demonstrate to these young people that I answer prayer," He seemed to say. "I'm going to show America that God is alive and still performs miracles. I'm going to bear witness to My own grace and power and purpose. I'll hear the cry of those who prayed and honor the faith of those who dared. Today I'm going to do something new."

What were the results of that rally? Only eternity will fully reveal what actually transpired. But once again God was saying that the day of mass evangelism was not over; the time was ripe. Pioneers had blazed the trail before. Evangelist Harry VanBrock . . . Dr. Percy Crawford . . . Jack Wyrtzen with his great rallies in Madison Square Garden. Now suddenly a spark became a fire, then a flame, a great conflagration.

From this great rally came a sweep across America, large meetings, in communities large and small. Multiplied tens of thousands, young and old, were swept into the Kingdom of God through faith in Jesus Christ.

For Billy Graham, Soldier Field, Memorial Day, 1945, became a source of inspiration. It gave impetus, through Dr. Robert P. Evans, to the Greater Europe Mission. It became a tower of aspiration to a Youth for Christ director, Bob Pierce of Seattle, to develop an organization now known as World Vision International. It was here that God spoke to Dr. Paul Freed, and Trans-World Radio became a reality, with more power in Christian radio than any other instrument of our time. Bob Cook moved on from music to preaching, to Christian publication, and eventually president of The King's College, Briarcliff Manor, New York. Bob Jones, Sr. and Jr., in the early struggling days of their college, received more students from Youth for Christ rallies than anywhere else. Everett Swanson established orphanages under the name of "Compassion." Hundreds and even thousands of young men and women on fire for God traveled to many places around the world where they effectively served Jesus Christ.

We prayed that God would give us good weather for a giant testimony to the saving grace of Jesus Christ. We didn't realize that God would not only answer prayer and give us a fruitful meeting but out of that meeting also would come added impetus, courage, faith, and energy in the lives of a multitude of people. They would live and serve and sacrifice, some, yea, to give up their lives, in a mighty movement of God which continues today in an ever-widening stream. Many organizations and fellowships, to the ends of the earth, testify to the faithfulness of God in answering prayer on that eventful day. To Him be the glory; great things He has done. We give God all praise. We are comforted to have been a small part of something big that God has done in our lifetime.

HAROLD LINDSELL has been editor of
Christianity Today since 1968. During the
previous year he served as Professor of Bible at
Wheaton College.

From 1964 to 1967 Dr. Lindsell was associate
editor of *Christianity Today*. Prior to that time, he
served in professorial positions at Fuller

Theological Seminary, Northern Baptist
Seminary, and Columbia Bible College.

A 1938 graduate of Wheaton College, Dr.
Lindsell received an A.M. in history from the
University of California in 1939, Ph.D. in history
from New York University in 1942, and D.D.
from Fuller Theological Seminary in 1964.

Dr. Lindsell is the author of a number of
books, including *The Battle for the Bible; The
World, the Flesh and the Devil; When You Pray; The
Church's Worldwide Mission* (editor); *Christianity
and the Cults; Harper Study Bible* (editor); *Daily
Bible Readings* (editor); *The Morning Altar;
Missionary Principles and Practice;* and others.

A trustee of Wheaton College, Westmont
College, and Gordon-Conwell Theological
Seminary, Dr. Lindsell is listed in *Who's Who in
America* and *Directory of American Scholars.*

He is a member of the American Historical
Association, American Society of Church History,
American Academy of Political and Social
Sciences, Pi Gamma Mu (social studies), Pi
Kappa Delta (forensics), and National
Association of Evangelicals.

Dr. Lindsell and his wife, the former Marion
Bolinder, have three married daughters. They
also have a married son, John.

The Day That Changed My Life
Harold Lindsell

Did I meet God? Or did God meet me? That
question haunts every believer when he seeks to
discern the workings of God in his life. Certainly
it was God who met Moses in the burning bush.
It was God who initiated the incident that was to
change Moses' life for the rest of his days. It was
God who came to Abraham in a vision and made
a covenant with him. It was God who entered
into the life of Jacob who wrestled with the
divine visitor who changed his name to Israel.
And it may well be that God has worked in my
life and in that of other Christians when I and
they have been conscious of it or not.

I recall with never-ending amazement one
experience I had with God, leading to a decision
that changed the whole course of my life from
that day to this. I doubt that I understood fully
how present God was when it happened. I do
not recall any sense of the luminous. There was
no burning bush, no dream, no ecstasy. But God
was at work, and in that experience He did
something so important for me and so moving
that when I reflect on it I am constrained to offer
unceasing praise.

The incident I am thinking of was the decision
to enter Wheaton College back in 1935. On the
surface such a decision may appear to have been
relatively insignificant. I know that at the time I
did not realize its importance myself. I rather
doubt that Moses at the time had any full
appreciation of what the burning bush experience

was to mean to him across the years. I don't think Abraham, at the time it happened, envisioned what it meant to be the chosen one through whom God would bless mankind by making Jesus the Redeemer his offspring. In no way do I compare myself with these patriarchs of yesteryear, but there may be something similar about our experiences.

A word of background on my early life is necessary. I was a Christian when I applied for admission to Wheaton. I do not recall when first I was regenerated. I simply have no knowledge of the time, the place, or the circumstances. I only know that I have been a Christian as far back as I can remember. I was reared in a Bible-believing Presbyterian church. I confessed Christ publicly before the elders of the church when I was twelve. I joined the church and partook of the Lord's Supper for the first time. The church itself was theologically fundamental but sociologically liberal.

Matters like dancing, card playing, movies, tobacco, and alcohol were peripheral. I learned to play pinochle, bridge, and cribbage with my parents. If we wanted to go to the movies, we went. If we wanted to dance, we did. My brother took to tobacco. For some reason I never did, although I remember smoking a few cigarettes and one or two cigars.

Alcohol was not on the list of preferred beverages in my home and never became a habit or a problem to me or to my family. This social facet of my life was significant because the decision to attend Wheaton College brought into perspective the sociological fundamentalism of the school, a form of Christian life with which I was not well acquainted and concerning which I had had little or no teaching.

Following graduation from high school at sixteen I was faced with the great depression. It was 1930 and economically the nation was in the doldrums. I secured a job as an office boy in an insurance company and was promoted in due time to the workmen's compensation and public liability underwriting department. I attended the City College of New York at night, taking courses in economics and accounting.

When I was twenty I developed severe allergic reactions which, unknown to me at the time, came from dogs. The allergy triggered other physical reactions. I was subject to frequent and severe bronchial infections.

I resigned my job with the insurance company early in the summer of 1934 and went to the Catskill mountains for a year. I lived on a farm, the owner of which had two sons in whose company I spent my time riding horses, cutting firewood, collecting sap for making maple syrup, and engaging in other activities common to rural life. As a city boy it was a decided change from the sidewalks of New York.

While I was in the Catskills I decided that I wanted to get a college degree. My only sister was a Phi Beta Kappa from Hunter College in New York and she had set a standard for her younger brother to follow. I went about the matter quite pragmatically. Not knowing the cause of the asthmatic attacks (those were the days before antihistamines) I assumed that climate might be at the root of the problem. So I investigated colleges far removed from New York. I wrote for catalogs from Washington State College in Pullman, Washington, and from other places where I thought the weather might be salubrious. Then one day a strange thing happened.

The owner of the farm where I was a paying guest ran what was essentially a boarding house, largely for summer vacationers. But some guests occasionally came to the mountains during the winter, late fall, and early spring. At that time there was little or no attention paid to winter skiing.

Several people from New Jersey came to spend a long weekend at the farm. One man, a Plymouth Brethren, whose name I have since forgotten, engaged me in conversation. I told him I intended to go to college. He suggested that I seriously consider Wheaton College. I had never heard of the school, nor did I have the slightest idea of what it might be like. He supplied me with the address of the college and made me promise that I would write for a catalog. I agreed to do so and I followed through on my promise. I did not really know then, although it was to become plain to me in later years, that God was at work in my life in a singular fashion of which I had only the dimmest awareness.

The Wheaton College catalog arrived and I read it through. It looked like a good school and I was attracted by its obvious Christian emphasis. The catalog was clear enough about one aspect of the college's life: smoking, drinking, gambling, card playing, movies, dancing, and secret societies were forbidden. This cut right across my sociological liberalism. But that had not been a consuming passion and presented no formidable problem. I took a hard look at the application blank. Among the questions it asked was whether I had ever read the Gospel of John through at one sitting. I hadn't. I sat down and did so. I could then respond affirmatively to the question. I agreed to keep the parietal rules too.

And I sent in the application for admission.

My decision to apply for admission to the college did not come after a period of extended prayer, nor was it brought about by some supernatural religious experience. It was simply a sense of oughtness, a subjective feeling that it was the right thing to do. Certainly at that time I was no daily or avid reader of the Bible. I did know the Bible as well as the average church-going young person of my day. I could repeat the books of the Bible in order without error. I had committed a number of Bible verses to memory in Sunday school, and daily vacation Bible school; I had participated in many Bible drills. I had attended innumerable Christian Endeavor meetings and had been exposed to situations where the Bible was used and believed. In my family everyone went to Sunday school and church. The only excuse for missing either was illness. We sat in a family pew together until I was in my middle teens.

The test of the presence of God is to be found not simply in an experience, but also in what happens *after* the experience or the decision. I arrived at Wheaton, a 21-year-old young man from the big city. My peers were right out of high school. Many of them came from rural areas. Some from the South came from environments quite different from that of the New York City dweller.

Margaret Bailey Jacobsen tells about an incident I do not remember. One day I was seated by the hostess in the college dining hall alongside Margaret and her friend Eizabeth Walker, who later married Ken Strachan. Apparently this New Yorker so upset these young ladies from the South that following the dinner table discussion they went to their room and held a prayer meeting on my behalf! Margaret told me later she felt that anything I have done for Christ and His Kingdom flowed out of that prayer meeting by these two utterly sincere girls who had my best interests at heart. Maybe she's right.

I did not like Wheaton at all. I had no trouble academically; I came to college for an education. Indeed I was impressed that, attending Wheaton whose rules proscribed some social activities, I would have nothing to do but study. Before the end of the first semester I had made up my mind I would leave the college. I wrote to my parents. Their reply was simple. "*You* made the choice to go to Wheaton. What are you complaining about?" Following the Christmas vacation I returned for the end of the first semester. I decided it would be better to finish out the year, which I did.

At the beginning of the second semester we had mid-year revival services. This one in 1936 certainly was one of the great visitations of the Spirit of God at Wheaton. It was all of that in my life. I got turned around, and I began to enjoy the college. There was nothing wrong with the school. There had been something wrong with me. When I got some of my spiritual priorities straightened out things were different.

I went home at the end of my first year and could hardly wait for the sophomore year to begin. It was the seal of God on a decision that had been made in the Catskills when God was really very present in my life even though the awareness of that presence was hazy and inexplicit. But the story does not end there. That decision, part of the sovereign operating providence of God in my life, changed the course of my journey in ways I could not have envisioned when God first led me to apply for admission to the college.

When I came to Wheaton I intended to pursue a business major. I wanted to make a lot of money. I was led instead to major in history. I graduated in 1938, and went on to take a Ph.D. in that discipline at New York University. I needed a teaching job. I had met and heard Robert McQuilkin in the 1936 revival at Wheaton. The summer following the acquisition of the doctorate I wrote 108 letters looking for a teaching post. Nothing opened up. At the end of the summer I got a letter from Wheaton telling me of an opening at Columbia Bible College, one school I had not written to.

I met Dr. McQuilkin at the Pennsylvania Railroad station in New York City on Labor Day, 1942. The next day I was on my way to Columbia, South Carolina. It was there that I met and married Marion Bolinder. Had I not gone to Wheaton I would not have met Dr. McQuilkin. Nor would I have gone to Columbia Bible College. Nor would I have met and married Marion.

While studying for the M.A. degree at the University of California at Berkeley (1938; the degree was received in 1939) I visited the home of my uncle in Seattle, Washington. My birthday comes on December 22. At Wheaton I had met Rosa and Ruth Bell. Ruth, who later married Billy Graham, sent me a book for my birthday in 1938. It was Oswald Chamber's classic *My Utmost for His Highest.*

While I was reading that book, the Spirit of God met me in a new way. I surrendered my life to Christ for His will and His service. So when I came to Columbia Bible College it was with a new commitment to Jesus Christ. But had I not

gone to Wheaton, I would never have met the
Bell sisters, and Oswald Chambers might still be
an unknown author to me.

I met Carl F. H. Henry at Wheaton. He was
responsible for recommending my name to
Northern Baptist Theological Seminary for a post
in church history and missions. Later he and I
were among the first four faculty members of the
Fuller Theological Seminary which opened its
doors in 1947. I recommended him to L. Nelson
Bell and Billy Graham for the post of editor of
Christianity Today. Later I was to become
associate editor of the magazine. And following
Dr. Henry's resignation from the magazine, the
Board named me to succeed him.

My wife Marion's brother was in the air force
in World War II. He visited his sister at
Columbia Bible College before he was shipped
overseas. Marion and I introduced him to Jean
Wiggs whose grandfather was the famed R. A.
Torrey. Bob Bolinder later married Jean. She
and Bob as well as all of their children and all of
my children have gone to Wheaton College and
graduated from the institution. The second
generation met and married lads and lassies from
the college too.

I served on the faculty of Wheaton for one
year. Since then I have served on the Board of
Trustees for a number of years. But everything I
have done and the various works I have engaged
in have all sprung from that initial decision to
attend Wheaton.

As I look back I know that God met me at
that time in my life. It was a focal point that
turned me along the road He wanted me to
follow. What is more important, I can say that in
the decisions I have made at subsequent
important junction points of life since then there

has been a conscious awareness that God was
present. And I have had the assurance that what
was dimly incipient when I opted for Wheaton
had become a living reality. On many occasions I
have been met by God in beautiful ways that
have verified for me the greatness and the glory
of that early crucial moment when, in the
providence of God, I was led according to His
will.

The last great moment when I sensed a special
meeting with God occurred in December of
1975. I was attending the meetings of the World
Council of Churches in Nairobi. They were not
only dull; they were devoid of any spiritual
vitality that could grip my heart. At no point was
I lifted up, nor did I experience that special
sense of God's presence.

Then one day toward the close of the
Assembly I went to the auditorium before one of
the meetings was scheduled to begin. Something
curious happened. The music at the Assembly
had been modern for the most part and did not
sound much like the hymnody of the church
through the ages. But someone at the piano
began playing one of the great hymns of the
Church while people were scurrying around.

At that moment something happened in my
heart. The sense of the divine presence
overpowered me. Tears came to my eyes. I was
lifted up before the mercy-seat of God in
transport and shared with Isaiah the thought:
"Holy, holy, holy is the Lord of hosts; the whole
earth is full of his glory." That memorable
encounter with God would never have occurred
without the earlier decisions that so dramatically
altered the quality and direction of my life.

W. STANLEY MOONEYHAM has been
president of World Vision International since
1969. During the five previous years he served
with the Billy Graham Evangelistic Association,
first as a special assistant to the evangelist and
then as vice-president of international relations.

Dr. Mooneyham has a B.S. degree from

Oklahoma Baptist University and an honorary Litt. D. from Houghton College. He is listed in *Who's Who in America* and *Who's Who in Religion.*

Recipient in 1973 of the Order of Civil Merit, highest award given to a non-Korean by the government of South Korea, Dr. Mooneyham has edited or authored a number of books.

Among these are *The Dynamics of Christian Unity* (Zondervan); *One Race, One Gospel, One Task* (World Congress on Evangelism official volumes); *Christ Seeks Asia* (Asia-South Pacific Congress on Evangelism official volume); *China: the Puzzle,* and *What Do You Say to a Hungry World?*

Dr. Mooneyham has held non-vocational positions with the National Sunday School Association (secretary, vice-president), National Association of Free Will Baptists (moderator), Evangelical Press Association (vice-president, president), *Decision* magazine (consulting editor).

Also Family Concern, Inc. (advisory board member), International Congress on World Evangelization (continuation committee member), and International Congress of Chinese Evangelicals (advisory council member).

Earlier vocational associations included *Shawnee,* Oklahoma, *News-Star* (reporter), First Free Will Baptist Church, Sulphur, Oklahoma (pastor), and National Association of Evangelicals (director of information, editor of *United Evangelical Action,* interim executive director).

A New Power Loose in the Land

W. Stanley Mooneyham

As our Cathay Pacific jet turned for the approach
into Pochentong Airport just outside Phnom
Penh, I saw clearly the markings of the Swissair
plane on the ground. Before leaving Hong Kong
three hours earlier, I had read in the *South China
Morning Post* of the planned departure of the
Chinese diplomatic delegation from Cambodia
following the fall of the Sihanouk regime.

The Boeing 707 bearing the red cross emblem
of the neutral European nation obviously was
there for the flight to Peking.

After the pilot had taxied and parked our
Convair 880, the ground crew nudged a stairway
against its side and I stepped out into the stifling
humidity of Southeast Asia. I was back in
Cambodia, now aflame with war, at the request
of the new government to discuss humanitarian
assistance to the suffering people.

It was ironic. Just five years after Prince
Sihanouk had thrown out the last American
Protestant missionaries, Drew Sawin, son of
missionaries in South Vietnam, had arranged
with the new government for another Christian
organization to be invited back.

We were met by the appropriate government
officials and, as the head of our little party, I was
treated like a diplomat. I remembered Paul's
words, "Now then we are ambassadors for
Christ" (2 Corinthians 5:20). This was not

entirely inappropriate, for just as I emerged from
our plane, the Chinese ambassador—with a
magnificent sense of timing, I thought—stepped
into his plane! The scene was right out of a
Hollywood movie. I sensed something of the
significance of our mission, but at that moment I
knew nothing of what God would do in the next
five years or how I would be a part of it. I
remember feeling, however, that this country was
going to become a part of my life and that
somehow, some way, I would become a part of
the life of its people.

There was the certainty of being in God's
place at God's time.

It was May 1970. The seemingly endless
conflict in Vietnam had spilled over into the
peaceful villages of Cambodia. Unprepared both
physically and psychologically for this cruel
assault on its land and life, the ancient kingdom
of the Khmers tried to fight back. But the
response was pitiful. Placid, tucked-away
Buddhist kingdoms don't fight a lot, so there was
no trained army. No stockpiles of arms. Not
even uniforms or transportation. The young
soldiers recruited from the rice paddies rode to
the front in dilapidated Pepsi-Cola trucks.

The Khmer kings had once been fierce
warriors. Historically, the people themselves have
done their share of bloodletting—particularly
against the Vietnamese. But that was a long time
ago. Buddhism had since helped pacify the
people. The average Cambodian lived quietly, if
not richly. His peasant life moved at a tranquil
pace.

Now that quiet life had been shattered.
Invaders were shooting up the countryside and
terrorizing villages. Almost overnight the capital
city of Phnom Penh had become a fetid,

sprawling refugee camp. The hospitals, as one government official told me, were "little better than cowsheds." Everything was in short supply. Need was total. Because of the unpopularity of U.S. involvement, most organizations were turning a deaf ear to the nation's plea for help. Cambodia was a political liability.

We viewed it as an opportunity. That's why we were there. What I saw during those days as I moved in and out of burned villages, overcrowded hospitals and festering refugee camps is etched deeply in my memory. I felt God was talking to me through my eyes, and I couldn't help asking myself what it would mean to lose everything? To be forced from my home? To have my family shot up? To be denied a livelihood? To be a refugee?

As our team discussed how we might help, Larry Ward reminded me that our warehouse in Saigon was bulging with recently-arrived supplies. But we had no money for a plane to transport them. The only way to get those critically needed supplies to Phnom Penh was by road.

By road? It would either be one of the most foolhardy things I had ever participated in or it would be unmistakably part of some divine plan. Highway 1 between Saigon and Phnom Penh ran through a very dangerous area called the "Parrot's Beak." More than half of the 150-mile distance was under frequent ambush by the Viet Cong.

Could we make it? We didn't know. We knew only that we must try.

So that was how, after much prayer and discussion, we found ourselves in Saigon three days later loading a ten-ton truck with cots, crutches, wheelchairs, medical instruments, high

protein food supplement, and other priceless
supplies.

God seemed to say "go." I knew this did not
necessarily mean our safety was guaranteed.
Sometimes the purposes of God are better served
by our dying than by our living, but I had a
deep confidence that God's plan would be
accomplished.

What should have been a five-hour trip took
all day. It was as much a test of patience as of
faith. We fumed at bureaucratic delays; blitzed
the Vietnam/Cambodian border, only recently
opened, when a Vietnamese guard couldn't read
our passes written in Khmer; detoured around a
dozen dynamited bridges; sweated out more
terrifying situations than that.

And after anointing every foot of Highway 1
with prayer, we arrived in Phnom Penh just
thirty minutes ahead of sunset. God had been
with us. It had not gone so well with eight
correspondents on the previous day, we learned
on our arrival. They had been killed or captured
in the Cambodian countryside.

Again I had the feeling that God was
arranging something beyond my knowledge.

Relief officials in the new government planned
a public ceremony the next morning when we
turned over the supplies to them. When asked to
say something, I used the opportunity to speak of
the love of God which had motivated us to serve
suffering humanity. These Buddhist officials
smiled and nodded approvingly. I spoke of the
sacrificial love of Jesus Christ. It was probably the
first time in the history of the country that Name
had been spoken in an official government
ceremony. There was no resentment.

We gave out no tracts nor distributed any
Bibles then. It would have seemed grossly

insensitive at that moment. We had been moved to share with a suffering people at this time of their need and, with no spiritual awareness, they viewed their greatest needs as medicines and hospital supplies. But even more, they needed to know that someone cared about them.

The other would come later. You see, I have discovered that love talked about can be easily turned aside, but love demonstrated is irresistible. From those early, spontaneous demonstrations of Christian love, other opportunities for service quickly developed. The new government also welcomed back the missionaries, so we began to work with the Christian and Missionary Alliance in a program of evangelism and relief. Into this partnership also came the small and struggling Khmer Evangelical Church—the only Protestant church in the country at that time—which began to emerge from its persecuted state.

The country was solidly Buddhist—virtually 100 percent. There were less than 500 Protestants out of a population of some 7 million people. Catholics numbered about 50,000, but most of these were French and Vietnamese. Little by little, however, the long-held hostility against Christianity began to melt away.

Cambodia was opened to the gospel by a ten-ton truck filled with love!

We were given many opportunities to be bold in our witness for Jesus Christ. The leadership of the national church took courage in their new freedom and formed their own relief and evangelistic teams. As love had opened the nation, so now it began to open many individual hearts. It was an exciting time to be God's person in Cambodia.

At the invitation of the national church and

with the permission of the Khmer government, I agreed to conduct in April 1972 the first public evangelistic campaign ever held in the country. Church leaders decided to schedule the meetings to coincide with the Cambodian new year. This was a three-day holiday, and for the occasion the government gave us use of the 1,500-seat Moha Srop Tonle Basac auditorium on the edge of the Tonle Sap River. Soldiers were also dispatched to search each person coming into the building to protect us against sabotage.

None of us knew what to expect. Ten people might show up. Or a thousand. Never in our wildest imagination were we prepared for the thousands who had to be turned away on the first day. We were astounded. The meetings had been announced as "Good News for the Khmer People" and thousands pushed and shoved for seats to hear what we had to say.

There was a choir of about forty young people. Thirty counselors had been trained. (I thought that was probably twice the number needed.)

I was both exhilarated and frightened as I walked to the platform with my interpreter, Son Sonne, secretary of the Cambodian Bible Society. To my mind, the gospel I had preached for twenty-five years was about to be put to the most severe test of my ministry. I preached the simplest sermon of my life. It started with God and creation and ended forty-five minutes later with Calvary and the resurrection. Scores walked out scoffing as I spoke of the virgin birth, the miracles of Jesus, and His resurrection.

This was not the "good news" they had come to hear. As never before, I saw how "foolish it sounds to those who are lost, when they hear that Jesus died to save them" (1 Cor. 1:18). I

confess, however, that what little confidence I
had when the meeting started was severely
shaken. Everything I had learned earlier from the
church leaders and the missionaries had prepared
me for little or no response. I knew it was a
cultural fact that to a Cambodian "to be different
is to be wrong," and I was asking them to
change centuries of religious belief.

With trepidation—almost embarrassment at the
certainty of "failure"—I invited the people to
turn from their idols, believe in the living God,
and receive his Son, Jesus Christ, as Lord and
Savior. Neither Son Sonne nor I nor anyone else
was prepared for what happened.

Almost half the audience—over 500
people—stood immediately! I thought they had
misunderstood. Son Sonne and I went over the
invitation again very carefully. Then we asked
those who misunderstood or were not serious in
their response to be seated. Only a handful took
their seats.

I was still incredulous. True, I had spoken
God's Word, but I refused to believe the miracle
I was seeing. It was not possible. It had never
happened before. I tried to find ways to separate
the "earnest seekers" from the "insincere"—my
categories. Almost all the original number stayed
with me all the way. Right through coming to
the front of the auditorium and even up onto the
platform! Finally, there was nothing to do except
ask our thirty counselors to take groups of up to
twenty persons and instruct them from the
Scriptures. Only when I saw these groups
gathered all over the auditorium reading the
Word of God did the truth penetrate my
"psyched up" defeatist mentality.

I had been a spectator to a miracle of God,
and had not believed it. So devastating was that

awareness that I went over to a corner of the platform and sat down and wept, asking God to forgive my unbelief.

The next day the scene was repeated, except that this time we had arranged a public address system outside the auditorium for the overflow crowd. I preached the same sermon inside and outside with similar response.

"I wouldn't believe this unless I had seen it with my own eyes," said Minh Tien Voan, an engineering graduate of the University of Georgia and chairman of the counseling committee. "One time," he told me, "I tried to get into the meeting and a young man standing there wouldn't let go of me. I thought he wanted to go inside, but I told him there were no more seats. He insisted he didn't want to go in. He just wanted to become a Christian. So I led him to Christ right there on the steps."

The third day was no different.

It was a breakthrough for which no man could take credit. Not only were we totally unprepared for it; we didn't believe it when it happened.

For nearly half a century, the Cambodian Protestant Church had been a church of the shadows. They had been beaten down, imprisoned, despised. Then almost overnight the situation changed. The name of Jesus could be spoken in public. Christians were no longer ashamed and afraid. They began to witness as never before. Bible study groups were formed all over the city and in refugee camps. Buddhist priests came to the homes of missionaries and asked about Jesus.

Chau Uth, president of the Khmer Evangelical Church, told me: "We feel Phnom Penh has been shaken, turned upside down. Before, we were a hidden people, but now we are visible."

Six months later I was invited to return for a

working. Now the choir numbered over 100.
Scores of new converts had been trained as
counselors.

This time several high officials responded to
the message of Christ. A missionary said he had
been praying for one official for fifteen years.
When the man stood during the invitation, the
missionary went to him and talked with him
about his needs—particularly about his need for a
Savior. The official prayed and asked Christ to
change his life.

The head of the Supreme Court asked to see
me in my hotel room. He told me he had been a
secret believer ever since someone had given
him a New Testament many years before. Now
he wanted to publicly identify with the
Christians.

For many Cambodians, the fact that even a
fledgling Khmer Protestant church existed at all
came as quite a shock. The seed-sowing of fifty
years of missionary witness had dramatically
sprung forth with new life. Now thousands heard
the good news: *Jesus loves you very much.* He died
to bring peace, not only to a troubled country,
but to troubled minds. Jesus will accept you
where you are. No conditions. You do not need
a Buddhist begging bowl to make you good
enough to earn God's favor. You are already
loved. Christ died for you because He loves you.
Believe it and live.

And believe it they did.

I know there were many reasons why the
people responded so readily to the gospel. For
one thing, war and possible death had caused

many to think about eternity. Among young
people, there was frustration with a government
that couldn't pull it all together. A threadbare
Buddhism that no longer met real needs had
deprived thousands of intellectuals of any
spiritual hope. Many uprooted refugee peasants
were responding to the tangible acts of love
shown to them by Christians, both foreign and
Khmer.

But underneath it all, I know that it was God's
time for Cambodia. There can be no other
reason for a spiritual explosion as dramatic as was
witnessed between 1972 and 1975. The work of
God continued to grow spectacularly until the
spring of 1975 when the country fell to the
Communists. No one knows how many
Christians there were. Certainly thousands. They
were multiplying too rapidly to count them and
there were not enough churches to absorb them
or pastors to train them. In Phnom Penh alone,
the number of churches in those three years had
grown from four to twenty-eight.

For the time being, Cambodia is off limits. The
new rulers have drawn down a curtain of silence
around the country. My passport no longer gets
its regular stamp at Pochentong Airport. I no
longer have the privilege of loving my
Cambodian friends face to face, but I haven't
stopped loving them. And I still consider myself
an adopted son of the land, whether the new
regime likes it or not.

The Khmer church has likely gone
underground again. But it is a much bigger
underground. Those thousands of refugees who
came from the countryside to Phnom Penh and
there met Jesus the Christ, have now gone back
to their villages with their new Friend. What we
saw between 1972 and 1975 may have been only

the lighting of the fuse. The real explosion of God's power may be an event yet for the future in Cambodia.

As God knew the future and had a plan in 1970, so He does today. I will be forever thankful that during the brief interlude of freedom in Cambodia, I had the opportunity to announce God's love to some of the most beautiful people on earth. A new power has been let loose in the land. It is the transforming power of Christ's love. Cambodia will never be the same.

Nor will I.

DR. HAROLD JOHN OCKENGA is
president of Gordon-Conwell Theological
Seminary, located on the north shore of Boston.
On April 1, 1976, he retired from the College
presidency to give his full time to the Seminary.
He now serves as chancellor of Gordon College.

Prior to his coming to Gordon in 1969, Dr.

Ockenga served as pastor of Boston's historic Park Street Church for 33 years.

A native of Chicago, Dr. Ockenga received his A.B. at Taylor University, his B.D. from Westminster, his M.A. and Ph.D. degrees from the University of Pittsburgh, in addition to which he has been awarded nine honorary degrees.

Dr. Ockenga occupied the pulpit of Westminster Chapel, London, as guest minister in 1946, '48, '51, and '64. He was one of the founders of the National Association of Evangelicals and the first president from 1942–44. Later he became Chairman of the International Commission of the NAE and President of the American Board of the World Evangelical Fellowship.

In 1947 he was a member of President Truman's Clergymen's Mission to Europe. He was co-founder and President of Fuller Theological Seminary, Pasadena, Calif., from 1947–54, and 1960–63, and served for extended periods as Chairman of the Board of Trustees.

He is presently chairman of the board of *Christianity Today* and a director of the Billy Graham Evangelistic Association. Dr. Ockenga is heard each Sunday morning over radio station WHDH in Boston where for more than 40 years he has taught the weekly International Sunday School Lesson.

He is the author of thirteen books, including *The Church in God, Protestant Preaching in Lent, Power Through Pentecost, Women Who Made Bible History* (recently reprinted by Zondervan), *Preaching in Thessalonians.* The Gordon Press produced two booklets of sermon collections since his presidency of Gordon under the titles: *No Other Lord,* and *Faith in a Troubled World.*

How God Healed Our Team *Harold John Ockenga*

Being filled with the Spirit was for me the
notable experience that transcended all other
memorable encounters with God. I have
experienced instantaneous healing from
sicknesses which would have cancelled the
usefulness of my ministry; I have known deep
spiritual visitations following acts of confession
and restitution; I have experienced times of mass
visitation of the Holy Spirit in preaching
conversion. But the most notable encounter with
God I have known is "Spirit filling," comparable
to the deeper experience of famous Christians.

I am glad to bear witness of this encounter
because great confusion exists in the Christian
church over what is called "the baptism of the
Holy Spirit" by the Pentecostals, or "the second
blessing" by the Holiness Movement, or "the
victorious life" by the Keswickian emphasis.
What each of these movements is seeking and
calls by different terminology, I believe the
Biblical term of "being filled with the Holy
Spirit" satisfies.

Earlier encounters with God were experienced
by me before being filled with the Spirit. One of
these occurred when I was only eleven years old
and had been taken with a dozen members of the
Sunday school class of my Chicago church to the
Des Plaines Campground by a Sunday school
teacher, who was a Chicago fireman. After a
week of camping, we attended a Sunday morning
service in the Des Plaines Tabernacle. Although

I cannot recall the preacher's name or his text or
his subject, I do know that the preached Word
touched my heart, and I, along with other young
people, presented myself at the altar in
repentance and faith in order to become a
Christian. Following that experience, I united
with the church, was sensitive to a spiritual
dimension in my life and both believed in and
sought to please the Lord Jesus Christ.

Six years later as I was graduating from high
school, the youth worker in the Chicago church
of which I was a member invited me to go to an
older boys' conference at Galesburg, Illinois,
with expenses paid by the church. I accepted the
invitation and attended the conference. It had an
indifferent effect upon me until the closing
service. Then a man called Daddy Gage
expounded the Scripture from 2 Samuel 23:15,
"David remarked, 'How thirsty I am for some of
that good water in the city well!' (The well was
near the city gate.)"

He told the story of David's three mighty men
breaking through the Philistine host, drawing
water out of the well, then fighting their way
through the Philistine host again to David.
Instead of receiving the water, David, looking
at the gourd and probably seeing a drop of
blood, poured the water out as a libation unto
the Lord and said, "No, my God, I cannot do it!
This is the blood of these men who have risked
their lives."

Daddy Gage then expounded to us the
sacrifice which Christ had made for us and the
need of our giving ourselves back to Him in
dedicated service. I responded by leaving the
meeting for my hotel room where I promised the
Lord I would dedicate my life to Him in
full-time service if He would meet the needs of

my heart spiritually. That night I bore my first testimony in a public service and have been serving the Lord ever since. Fifty years have not dimmed the glow of that encounter with God.

Shortly after that experience, the youth worker who was responsible for sending me to Galesburg began to persuade me to abandon my intention of going to Chicago University and to choose instead a small Christian college in Indiana called Taylor University. Since I had become a Christian under the leadership of this youth worker, and since she had begun to instruct me in Christian truths and practices, I responded affirmatively to her intercession. I matriculated in the spring term at Taylor University with the promise that if I didn't like it, all my expenses would be paid and I would be able to go to Chicago University in the fall.

Life at the Christian college was quite different from that in a secular Chicago high school of more than 7,000 students. I was in the midst of Christian students; I attended chapel every day; classes were commenced with prayer; opportunities were given for participation in public religious services; and the teaching fortified my Christian commitment and determination to serve the Lord. At the end of the term I voluntarily elected to return for what proved to be four years of Christian education.

In the second term of study I was invited to hold an evangelistic campaign for ten days. Permission was given by the Dean and I launched into the preparation of ten days of sermons in the Methodist church of a small Indiana town. This taste of evangelism was to turn the course of my life.

After the campaign a group of three of us began to pray together regularly about the

possibility of the Lord using us in evangelistic
work as a team. We met together weekly; we
accepted invitations to go out on weekends to
minister in small churches, and soon we saw the
need for a song leader and soloist. In answer to
prayer for such a person, God added the fourth
member to the team.

We plunged into a busy schedule of college
work and interests during the week with
evangelistic activity on the weekends. Three of
us on the team alternated the preaching
responsibility. One was charged with the musical
leadership and other responsibilities were
assigned according to ability. By spring we were
praying regularly that the Lord would lead us
into a summer evangelistic ministry. Invitations
came and following commencement, we launched
into our work.

We divided our days into times of devotion
and Bible study, a period of calling in the homes
of the farming communities, meetings for prayer
and evening evangelistic services. God honored
the effort with the conversion of young people
and many older people. Our meetings usually
lasted about ten days.

After several of these campaigns, we came to a
small town called La Gro, Indiana, where our
meetings were to be held in the local
Presbyterian church. The team was quartered in
a large farmhouse some distance outside of the
town. Each morning after breakfast the team
would go to town and take different rooms in
the church for personal study of the Bible and
for audible prayer. If, for any reason, we had a
division of opinion, or any problem, we would
begin with a prayer meeting for the four of us in
the church where the meetings were being held,
and would tarry there most of the night in prayer.

Following one of the evening services, a team member asked me if he could take a walk with me. As we walked together he said, "I think the team is going to break up."

I asked him how. He pointed out a number of ways in which I had caused irritations for members of the team, matters of insensitivity and unconcern of other people's welfare and rights.

I didn't want to see that, so I said to the brother, "What shall I do?" He took the forefinger of his right hand and pointed it into the corner of my shoulder. "Ockenga," he said, "you are coming, but you haven't arrived yet. You had better go out and pray all night."

I took his advice, but not as he had expected it. I got up earlier in the morning each day and prayed about my own problem, the hunger in my own life and the need of the team. A few days later another preaching member of the team asked to take a walk with me; he told me very much the same things. This intensified greatly my own spiritual hunger and sense of frustration.

Our college was of Methodist association and taught the doctrine of entire sanctification in the Wesleyan tradition. There was no question in the minds of the other members of the team or of myself that I was a Christian, that my sins had been forgiven, that I had been called to the ministry and that I was preaching the gospel, but they did not believe that I had become sanctified. Later theological reflection caused me to reject the teaching of the eradication of sin. This merely emphasized to me the necessity of a truly overcoming life, as promised in Scripture.

Being seriously committed to the Lord and being called to preach, I dedicated a great deal of time to prayer and Bible study over this problem. An inner conviction told me there were

areas of my life which were not under the
Lordship of Christ; there were practices out of
harmony with Biblical holiness. Now that other
people saw this same thing, I would have to deal
with them. Therefore, I came to the place in
prayer where I told the Lord repeatedly if He
didn't do something for me spiritually, I would
leave the ministry for I would not preach about
something that I did not experience.

After several sessions such as that, Sunday
arrived. Though not scheduled to preach, I sat
on the platform with the team, and participated
in the service. I expected the Lord to bless the
sermon which was on the subject: "Ye shall have
power after that the Holy Ghost is come upon
you." At the conclusion of the sermon, our team
member speaker gave the invitation. I had heard
him preach that sermon before and had seen
many people respond to the invitation. This time
no one responded. He announced that the last
verse of the hymn would be sung once more and
the benediction would be pronounced.

An objective but internal voice said to me,
"Do you want that blessing?"

I responded, "Yes, Lord, but not here."

On Friday night, I had preached to that
congregation and thirteen people had responded
to accept Christ as Saviour. But I had a
consciousness that the Lord meant business and I
had told Him that I meant business. Just before
the speaker pronounced the benediction, I
tapped him on the shoulder. Sharing my
testimony with the people, I told them I was
going down to that altar to ask God to do
something for me internally and spiritually which
I desperately needed. Walking to the front, I
knelt at the altar. Others came also.

In the prayer meeting that followed, waves of

emotion broke over me and others. When I looked up through the tears, that first member of the team who had put his finger in the corner of my shoulder said with a smile, "Well, I think it's done, isn't it?" I replied, "I think it is."

My relationship to the team changed; a new victory in my personal life came; power in preaching and a new understanding of Biblical and Christian things increased from that day forward. The team stayed together for three years, preaching throughout the Northeast with great blessing and wonderful rewards. God had healed the breach in the team by doing something in my own life. The preaching members all went on into the ministry.

As for me personally, this was the experience of being filled with the Holy Spirit. From that time on, I had assurance as to the Spirit-filled life. With St. Paul I could say, "I know that when I come unto you, I shall come in the fullness of the blessing of Christ."

The intensity of the encounter with the Lord has not always remained the same. By neglect or disobedience, I have grieved the Spirit at times. But for fifty years, in the proportion that I have met the New Testament prerequisites of the Spirit-filled life, the intensity of God's presence has been maintained.

Confession of not being filled with the Spirit, consecration of all unto Jesus Christ, prayer to be filled with the Spirit, belief that God has provided such a quality of life for us, and obedience to the internal promptings of the Spirit—these are the conditions for Holy Spirit filling. In the proportion that any believer meets these prerequisites, he too may have an encounter with God which is equated in the New Testament with the Spirit-filled life and results in unction, giving purity of heart, clarity of mind, and power in endeavor.

"But you are not like that, for the Holy Spirit has come upon you, and you know the truth. . . . But you have received the Holy Spirit and he lives within you, in your hearts, so that you don't need anyone to teach you what is right. For he teaches you all things, and he is the Truth, and no liar; and so, just as he said, you must live in Christ, never to depart from him" (1 John 2:20, 27).

DR. STEPHEN F. OLFORD is the
president and minister-at-large of Encounter
Ministries, Inc., a Christian organization
committed to reaching the world and preaching
the Word through radio, television, cassettes,
literature, as well as pulpit and platform
appearances.

For fourteen years Dr. Olford was pastor of the historic Calvary Baptist Church in New York City. During this time his voice was heard over radio around the world on "The Calvary Church Hour," and in strategic cities across North America on his television program, "Encounter."

In 1973 he relinquished the pastorate for a worldwide ministry in mass communication, pastors' seminars, Christian Life conventions, and church-centered Bible conferences.

Born of missionary parents, Olford spent his boyhood days in Angola, West Africa, where he witnessed the transforming power of the gospel among the A-Chokwe people. Later, as a result of a spiritual crisis, he yielded his life to God for the ministry.

Following his theological training in England, he served as an Army Scripture Reader in World War II, and then as an itinerant evangelist on both sides of the Atlantic. In 1953 he became the Minister of Duke Street Baptist Church in London, where he pastored until God called him to Calvary Baptist Church, New York.

In 1966 Wheaton College honored him with the degree of Doctor of Divinity, and in the same year Houghton College conferred on him the Doctor of Letters. Dr. Olford has authored numerous books, booklets and articles, including such titles as *The Secret of Soul-Winning, The Tabernacle: Camping with God, The Grace of Giving,* and *The Christian Message for Contemporary Man.*

He is married to the former Heather Brown, who is his helpmeet in the ministry and the mother of two sons, Jonathan and David.

When the Spirit Became Lord
Stephen F. Olford

Biblical truth and personal experience have
taught me that normal growth in the Christian
life not only implies but involves spiritual crises.
Indeed, there is a sense in which every act of
obedience constitutes a crisis. And it is also true
that, for a variety of reasons, some crises are
more memorable than others.

My conversion, on the occasion of my seventh
birthday, in Angola, West Africa, was a
memorable crisis. Several days before this I was
on trek with my missionary parents. On the last
lap of the journey I had a frightening experience.
One of the men, carrying my hammock,
stumbled while crossing a narrow bridge over a
fast-flowing stream. The hammock turned over,
ejecting me into the air—and on my way to a
watery grave. In God's providence, however, I
was caught by my clothes in an overhanging tree.
When eventually I was extricated, I knelt,
trembling, on the nearby bank to thank God for
my deliverance. I knew, even as I prayed, that I
was not prepared to meet my Maker.

Shortly after this I did encounter Jesus Christ
as my Lord and Saviour. Something my mother
said at family prayers sent me to bed troubled.
At midnight I called her to my bedside and said,
"I am not ready to meet Jesus; can you tell me
how?" Thank God, she did—and peace flooded
my soul.

My baptism, in a dammed-up pool, before

hundreds of national believers, was a memorable crisis.

My restoration from a period of backsliding was a memorable crisis. In fact, this return to the Lord consummated in my call to the ministry. At this time I was back in England, studying to be an engineer. But God made it abundantly clear that His plan for my life was to serve Him as a preacher—anywhere, at any time, and at any cost.

Following theological and missionary training, I was commissioned to "the work of an evangelist" (2 Tim. 4:5). Then came the seven years of World War II, when as an Army Scripture Reader I witnessed to thousands of men and women in the Forces, stationed or passing through Newport, Monmouthshire. Those were days of darkness, danger, and discipline, but I praise the Lord for them! Not only were souls saved and lives changed; my own faith was tested and strengthened.

Strangely, at this point in my spiritual history I became increasingly aware of a deep inner dissatisfaction. Something was missing. My soul hungered and thirsted for the presence of God and the power of His Spirit.

This awareness of need was intensified by something I saw, something I read, and something I felt. What I saw was a local movement of the Spirit in south Wales which greatly challenged me. A relatively unknown pastor-evangelist was being mightily used of God. Under his preaching supernatural things were happening which I could not dispute nor deny. The spirit of revival was abroad. All this created a yearning in my heart to see miracles take place under my own ministry of the Word.

Concurrently with this, I was encouraged to

read the lives of two men who had always captivated my interest. One was an evangelist, the other a pastor. The evangelist was D. L. Moody. I discovered that there was a period in his life when he longed to be "fully consecrated" to God. Already he was an internationally known evangelist, and, judged by others, he was riding high on a tide of blessing. Inwardly, however, he was hungry for more.

Two women in his church in Chicago recognized his need and started to pray for him. They told him, "You need the power of the Spirit." Then one day, in the city of New York, it happened!

Recalling this crisis, Moody says: "I cannot describe it, I seldom refer to it; it is almost too sacred an experience to name. Paul had an experience of which he never spoke for fourteen years. I can only say that God revealed Himself to me, and I had such an experience of His love that I had to ask Him to stay His hand. I went to preaching again. *The sermons were not different; I did not present any new truths; and yet hundreds were converted. I would not now be placed back where I was before that blessed experience if you should give me all the world . . ."* (author's italics).[1]

Then there was the biography of that distinguished preacher and pastor, F. B. Meyer. I had read most of his books and had been enriched by the instructional and devotional depths of his expositions. But once again, a specific paragraph from his story by A. Chester Mann arrested me.

It was at the Keswick Convention where F. B. Meyer "got his first glimpse of fully surrendered service, and where he yielded himself obediently

1. James Gilchrist Lawson, *Deeper Experiences of Famous Christians* (Anderson, In.: Warner Press, 1911), pp. 345–348.

to the heavenly vision. *Meyer had to acknowledge that, during the earlier years of his ministry, his service was without power with God or special favor with man. Then there came that moment when he saw the emptiness of mere service, and cried to God . . . to take supreme control of his life, guiding and directing . . . his every plan. From this time on, God ACCEPTED his service . . .*"[2] (author's italics and capitalization).

In my study of these men, I was particularly impressed with the fact that their enduement with power came after years of "fruitful" service for God. I remembered how Jesus talked about "fruit," "more fruit" and "much fruit"; but it was the *much fruit* that glorified the Father (John 15:2, 4, 8).

Up until now, I had been content with "fruit," or possibly "more fruit"; but what I had seen and read deepened what I now felt. I wanted "much fruit," to be sure; but more than this, I wanted *freedom* to be and to do all that would glorify the Father. I was fettered and frustrated in my Christian service, and I longed for the liberating power of the Spirit.

This led to action. Clearing my calendar for a period of two weeks, I decided to retreat to some quiet place to read and wait upon the Lord. I made arrangements to stay at a little cottage in Porthcawl, on the south coast of Wales. I took with me two suitcases of books, including the works of Calvin and Owen on the Holy Spirit. Titles of more modern writers were *Veni Creator* by Handley C. G. Moule, *The Spirit of God* by G. Campbell Morgan, *The Ministry of the Spirit* by A. J. Gordon, *The Holy Spirit of God* by Griffith Thomas, and others.

2. A. Chester Mann, *F. B. Meyer* (Old Tappan, N.J.: Revell, 1929), p. 106.

I also scheduled a study of such portions of Scripture as John 14–16, the Acts of the Apostles, Romans Chapter 8, 1 and 2 Corinthians, Galatians, and Ephesians. Morning, noon, and night I read, meditated, and prayed. Gradually confusions were clarified and convictions were crystallized.

But theology was not enough. There was still an unspeakable desire in my soul to be set free. Then one afternoon, while reading the Epistle to the Ephesians, I observed in a new way that all the blessings of the Spirit are *already* given to us in Christ.

Paul says: "Blessed be the God and Father of our Lord Jesus Christ, who hath blessed us with all spiritual blessings (or all the blessings of the Spirit) in heavenly places in Christ" (Eph. 1:3). This includes the incoming of the Spirit (1:13, 14), the indwelling of the Spirit (2:18), the enabling of the Spirit (3:16, 17) and the uniting of the Spirit (4:3).

As I pondered these verses, I was overwhelmed with the revelation of the *divine fullness* (Eph. 1:23, 3:19, 5:18) which was mine in Christ. Jesus died for my sins, rose again for my justification, and then ascended to heaven to bestow on me "the blessings of the Spirit." This I now appreciated more clearly. However, it was one thing to *appreciate* "the blessings of the Spirit," but quite another matter to *appropriate* them. There was still another chapter in this precious letter—and a liberating fullness awaiting me!

So I came to Ephesians 5 and verse 18, and God opened my eyes! In that familiar verse, Paul exhorts the saints at Ephesus who *already* knew the incoming, the indwelling, the enabling, and the uniting of the Spirit not to be "drunk with wine, wherein is excess; but to be filled with the Spirit." It was quite obvious that here was a conscious, continuous, and conspicuous experience in the Spirit for pastors and members, husbands and wives, parents and children, servants and masters. The question was how to know this fullness initially, and then to know this fullness continually.

As I examined the text within its context and compared Scripture with Scripture, I was struck with the sheer simplicity of it all. First, there was *the initial acceptance of the Spirit's control*—"Be filled in the Spirit and with the Spirit."

To quote Handley Moule: "The Apostle in effect calls upon the believer to 'yield himself unto God' the Holy Spirit as to a Power and Presence already dwelling in living reality within him, but waiting, as it were, for the welcome of the soul to come forth from within and take entire possession of the whole circle and range of life."[3] The secret, to me, was the word "control." While the Holy Spirit is both contrasted and compared to wine, *He is essentially a Person, and to be filled with Him is to come under His CONTROL.*

This led me to 2 Corinthians 3:17, where Paul tells us that "the Lord is that Spirit: and where the Spirit of the Lord is, there is liberty"; or, "Where the Spirit *is Lord,* there is liberty." I had always accepted the deity of the Spirit, but I had never acknowledged His *Lordship.* I knew Jesus was Lord, and had owned that Lordship in an objective sense, *but now I saw that the Lordship of Christ could only be real TO me as the Holy Spirit was made Lord IN me. This was the crisis point in my search for freedom and fullness in my Christian life.*

3. Handley C. G. Moule, *Veni Creator* (Glasgow: Pickering and Inglis Ltd.), p. 218.

Without reading further, I dropped to my knees and yielded everything to the reign and rule of the *indwelling* Spirit. No glory filled the room, no vision filled my eyes, and no tongues were uttered; but I knew, there and then, that *I was set free!* The fetters and frustrations were gone. I hadn't to wait to preach to know that I was liberated! There were tears in my eyes, but peace in my soul!

I turned to the Scripture again, only to confirm that the initial acceptance of the Spirit's control must be matched by *the continual dependence on the Spirit's control.* The verb indicates a continuous experience—"Be ye being filled with the Spirit." To maintain this fullness of the Spirit, there must be a daily repentance of sin—"Grieve not the Holy Spirit" (Eph. 4:30), and there must be a daily obedience to Scripture, for God gives the Holy Spirit "to them that obey him" (Acts 5:32), and the net result is that "where the Spirit is Lord, there is liberty."

I was so caught up in the wonder of this encounter with God that I cut short my stay at Porthcawl by three days and returned to Newport to share the news! Later that week I spoke at a rally of young people in Cardiff. The large church was packed, and God moved in such power that I was there until midnight, dealing with seeking souls. There was an authority in preaching I had never known before.

The next appointment was a week of meetings at the Hildenborough Hall Conference Center, near London, under the directorship of the British evangelist, Mr. Tom Rees. Each day, I spoke on prayer in the morning, and on the Holy Spirit in the evening, and the Lord was pleased to send us "times of refreshing" from His presence.

Friday night we gathered for a period of
sharing, to be followed by a concluding message.
American visitors were with us on that occasion.
Among them was a young man by the name of
Billy Graham. As he heard the testimonies of
these young people who had entered into the
fullness of the Holy Spirit, and then listened to
my exposition of Ephesians 5:18, he walked up
to me, at the close of the service, with that
resolute look in his eyes and that determined
thrust of his jaw, and asked to know more.

We were unable to talk freely at the time, but
made arrangements to meet in Wales. There I
found that Billy was seeking for more of God
with all his heart; and he felt that I could help
him. For most of two days we were closeted at
Pontypridd's hotel with our Bibles open, turning
the pages as we studied passages and verses. The
first day Billy learned more secrets of the "quiet
time." The next, I expounded the fullness of the
Holy Spirit in the life of a believer who is
willing to bow daily and hourly to the
sovereignty of Christ and to the authority of the
Word. This lesson was so new to me that it
cascaded out, revealing bright glimpses of the
inexhaustible power of the love of God.

Billy drank it in so avidly that I scarcely
realized the heights and depths that his spiritual
life had reached already. At the close of the
second day we prayed, like Jacob of old laying
hold of God, and crying, "Lord, I will not let
Thee go except Thou bless me," until we came
to a place of rest and rejoicing. And Billy
Graham said, "This is a turning point in my life,
this will revolutionize my ministry." [4]

4. John Pollock, *Billy Graham: The Authorized Biography*
(Minneapolis: Billy Graham Evangelistic Association), pp.
38, 39.

As I drove home that night I thanked God for the day, in a little room in Porthcawl, south Wales, where the Spirit of life in Christ Jesus made me free from the law of sin and death. I realized, of course, that I had not "attained," nor was I already "perfect"; but I also realized that I had enjoyed a *foretaste* of what will one day be "the glorious liberty of the children of God." For me, that experience was my most memorable encounter with God.

Stephen F. Olford page 157

Since then I have come to see, with increasing clarity, *that liberty in the Holy Spirit is not freedom to do what I want, but power to do what I ought.*

This is beautifully illustrated in the life and ministry of Jesus. Prophecy became history when "the Holy Spirit descended upon Him in bodily form like a dove" (Luke 3:22 NASB) and in *the power of that anointing* He went forth "to preach the gospel to the poor . . . to proclaim *release* to the captives, and recovery of sight to the blind, to *set free* those who are downtrodden, to proclaim the favorable year of the Lord" (Luke 4:18 NASB). After completing this divine mission, He made possible, through His passion and triumph, a similar ministry for all who follow in His train. So He said to His disciples, "As my Father hath sent me, even so send I you" (John 20:21), and then empowered them with the Holy Spirit to accomplish the task.

By the grace of God I am following in this train! And until Jesus comes or calls, I will preach and teach that "where the Spirit is LORD, there is LIBERTY." Hallelujah!

DR. ALAN REDPATH was born in
Newcastle-upon-Tyne, England, and educated at
Durham School, trained as a chartered
accountant (C.P.A.) and moved to London to
work with Imperial Chemical Industries in that
capacity.

Converted at 19 years of age, he left business

after six years with I.C.I. to become an evangelist with the National Young Life Campaign in January 1937. He continued in this sphere for three years.

From 1940–53, Dr. Redpath served as pastor of Duke Street Baptist Church, Richmond, Surrey, England; 1953–62, pastor, Moody Memorial Church, Chicago; 1962–66, pastor, Charlotte Baptist Chapel, Edinburgh, Scotland.

After a severe illness Dr. Redpath resigned from a pastoral ministry, and since January, 1967 has been engaged in a worldwide missionary and convention ministry.

He has authored the following books: *Victorious Christian Living* (studies in Joshua); *Victorious Christian Service* (studies in Nehemiah); *Victorious Praying; The Making of a Man of God* (studies on David); *The Royal Route to Heaven* (studies in 1 Cor.); *Blessings out of Buffetings* (studies in 2 Cor.); *Faith for the Times* (studies in Isaiah; volumes I & II published, volume III pending).

When Disaster Became a Door
Alan Redpath

Saturday, September 5, 1964, was one of the rare occasions when we were all together as a family. We had just had lunch and a time of family prayer.

My daughter Meryl and her husband and two children were with us. She was completing her midwifery training in Edinburgh prior to leaving for the Central African Republic for their first term of service with the Africa Inland Mission.

My younger daughter, Caroline, my wife and myself had just returned from a summer holiday conference. I was due to conduct a wedding later that afternoon, so I retired to my study to arrange final details for it and to complete preparation for the following day's ministry at Charlotte Baptist Chapel.

Suddenly as I was writing I lost control of my hand. It wandered all over the paper. I called out to my wife; but in a few moments I had lost my speech, my right side was paralyzed, and I found myself unable to walk. So I was put to bed, and the doctor was called immediately.

I had little doubt as to what had happened, and he confirmed the verdict. It was a cerebral hemorrhage which, of course, might well have proved fatal, especially if it had been followed by another attack. I did not lose consciousness nor suffer any pain at that time. My mind remained quite clear, but I was completely helpless. My speech returned, at least in part, in a few days, and I was able to walk a little within two weeks, with help.

I was due to visit missionary conferences in
Southeast Asia in November. In fact, I had
secured my tickets and completed all vaccination
and other formalities. It was felt advisable to call
in a specialist, and he would not allow me to
travel without first having a thorough
examination in the hospital to discover the extent
of the damage. So I accepted his decision and
went through certain tests.

During one of these, a main nerve in the back
of my neck was damaged, with the result that my
diaphragm was put out of action and my left arm
went into shock. For some seven or eight weeks
I suffered intense pain. The specialist, however,
was able to confirm that a main artery taking
blood to the brain had snapped. He said I was a
"very lucky man," because the hemorrhage had
stopped just in time. Had it gone a fraction
further it would have proved fatal. He suggested
that I should forget further work, and take life
gently. If I were prepared to do this, he told me,
I could expect to live until I was ninety. If,
however, I insisted on going back into harness,
he thought I would probably have five years,
possibly ten, but would be most unlikely to make
seventy. This was due to a general hardening of
the arteries, though my blood pressure had
remained quite low and I had no trouble at all
with my heart.

Medically, therefore, I knew the worst, and
was left to go through the slow process of
convalescence. In an illness of this kind one's
inner defenses are knocked down, physically,
mentally, and spiritually. I was reduced to
childhood. Physically I could only walk with
difficulty; mentally I found it impossible to
concentrate or think clearly; spiritually I found
that I could not pray or read my Bible. It was

indeed a dark, grim experience.

There was another factor, however, which the doctors could not take into account. One of the most comforting things in this experience had been the letters, cablegrams, and telephone calls which came to our home, assuring me of the prayers of God's people. Among these was a phone call from Dr. Billy Graham in Nebraska the day after my stroke. Another was from Dr. Stephen Olford in New York. He had heard the news just as he went into the evening service, and was so distressed he called the whole congregation to prayer on my behalf. He set his alarm clock to awaken him at 3 A.M. on Monday morning—8 A.M. British time—and called me in what was, for him, the middle of the night. The love, thoughts, and prayers of hundreds of Christian people throughout the world were a tremendous encouragement. Our dear folk at Charlotte Chapel were kindness itself, and both my wife and I—in fact our whole family—felt the strength of Christian fellowship as never before in our lives.

But, I confess, my reactions to the illness were not the most spiritual. We often say from the pulpit, "We should never ask *why* in such an experience—only *what?*" In other words, not "Why has God allowed this?" but "What lessons can I learn from it?" I am afraid I found myself asking why very often. Why had God allowed this to happen to me in the midst of a busy life, and so early in a new pastorate when He was apparently giving real blessing, and the church was filled twice each Sunday?

These and other questions constantly entered my mind. I sank to depths of despair beyond description. For days I could do nothing but weep. At this time someone wrote to me saying that if only I had enough faith I could be healed immediately. I must confess such comments gave me little comfort. I did not question God's ability to work a miracle in this dramatic way, but there came into my mind the query, "Have I any right to expect Him to reverse the laws of nature, which He Himself created, simply for my benefit?"

What about the possibility that this illness was a chastening from heaven rather than an attack from hell? I recalled the words of 1 Corinthians 11:30–32, "That is why many of you are weak and sick, and some have even died. But if you carefully examine yourselves before eating you will not need to be judged and punished. Yet, when we are judged and punished by the Lord, it is so that we will not be condemned with the rest of the world."

Had the Lord made some mistake in permitting this illness? Is there *any* exception to the truth that "all that happens to us is working for our good if we love God and are fitting into his plans" (Romans 8:28)?

Then I found myself being attacked by tremendous temptation, the like of which I had not known for twenty years or more. It seemed that the devil took advantage of my helplessness to throw everything he had at me. Sinful thoughts, temptation to impurity, bad language were all the shattering experiences of those days. My wife and family suffered from having a husband and father who had reverted to childhood.

After weeks of darkness and complete despair I remember one day crying out to God, "O Lord, deliver me from this attack of the devil. Take me right home! I would rather be in heaven than stay here any longer, and know that the last memory my family would have of me would be of a man living like a cabbage. Please get me out of this situation!"

It was then, the first time for months, that it seemed the Lord drew very near to me, though I am sure He was very near all the time, even if I was unconscious of the fact. I had no vision of Him, or any dramatic touch of healing, but I do know that a deep conviction came to my heart, in which He said, "You have this all wrong. The devil has nothing whatever to do with it. It is Me, your Saviour, Who has brought this experience into your life to show you two things. First, this is the kind of person—with all your sinful thoughts and temptations, which you thought were things of the past—which you always will be, but for My grace. I have never intended to make you a better man. In the second place, I want to replace you with Myself, if you will only allow Me to be God in you, and admit that you are a complete failure, and that the only good thing about Alan Redpath is Jesus."

That, of course, was a truth which I have known in theory, and indeed had preached for some years. But now I know it in experience. "I know I am rotten through and through so far as my old sinful nature is concerned. No matter which way I turn I can't make myself do right. I want to but I can't" (Romans 7:18). How that verse lived in my life in a new way that day, and ever since!

Then as I looked back over the corridor of memory at the past twenty-five years of ministry in London, Chicago, and Edinburgh, it seemed a pattern had been developing in my life which I had imagined was spiritual: to "work like any slave for God's own Son." I never had a regular

day off a week, never had time for my family,
for I was always too busy in Christian work for
that. Sinful man that I am, I had imagined that it
was all so spiritual! The Lord showed me that I
was putting work before worship. The busyness
of a barren life had taken its toll, and my
priorities had become all wrong. Even my quiet
time and my Bible study had become less
disciplined than in former years, and this had all
built up tremendous pressure in the ministry
which God had given me.

Furthermore, I saw that I had become proud
of being orthodox in doctrine—a sound,
conservative evangelical, but not nearly so
concerned about my obedience to the doctrine
which I preached. How desperately easy it is to
demand a greater measure of obedience from a
congregation than one is prepared to give in
one's own life. How humiliating to make such a
discovery! Yet, further still, I realized that I had
become much more concerned about the
knowledge of truth than the knowledge of God;
much more interested in turning to my Bible to
find neat outlines for sermons than to seek food
for my own soul. Paul's great ambition was
"That I may know *Him*" (Philippians 3:10), *not*
"That I may know *truth.*" The Lord Jesus had
become a much more theoretical and doctrinal
Christ than a saving, experimental Christ day by
day in my life.

As I lay in bed with such reflections, how
ashamed I was that God had given me such
privileges, and I had been so neglectful of them.
How I thanked Him for being called aside for
stillness, and how I praised Him for suffering.
"The punishment that you gave me was the best
thing that could have happened" (Psalm 119:71).
He began giving me promises such as Psalm

138:7, 8: "Though I am surrounded by troubles, you will bring me safely through them. You will clench your fist against my angry enemies! Your power will save me. The Lord will work out his plans for my life—for your lovingkindness, Lord, continues forever. Don't abandon me—for you made me." Then Psalm 118:17, 18: "I shall not die, but live to tell of all his deeds. The Lord has punished me, but not handed me over to death." A wonderful sense of peace came into my heart.

Somehow the tensions and strain of the years seemed to roll away from me. I was still desperately weak, but from that time on I began to experience the Divine touch of His healing hand. Slowly, but surely, gently and lovingly, He restored me to health and strength. Oh yes, there were long months when patience was tested and faith tried to the limit. But I saw perfectly clearly that the Lord's chastening hand had been upon me, for a purpose which could only be revealed through the experience which I had endured.

> *From sinking sands He lifted me;*
> *With tender hand He lifted me;*
> *From shades of night to plains of light,*
> *O praise His Name, He lifted me!*

As I looked back upon it all, I would not have missed it for anything that the world could give me. If the Lord had healed me dramatically and instantly, what blessing I would have missed! When I cried, He strengthened me with might in my soul. Without reversing the laws which He Himself created, He allowed them to work on my behalf in the richest experience of spiritual, mental, and physical recovery. I praise Him with all my heart.

When I saw the specialist some time later he

was absolutely amazed. He said that he had
never known anybody who had suffered such
damage to recover so completely. He could not
find one symptom of my illness left, apart from
slight damage to my right hand which still does
not work very well for writing, a very minor
matter—but perhaps a constant reminder of what
had been for me a Peniel experience when "I
saw God face to face and my life was preserved."

What the specialist could not be expected to
understand, I could see clearly: hundreds of
people had been praying for me. The Lord had
chastened me sore; the Holy Spirit had spoken to
me and shown me the danger of a life lived with
wrong priorities, and I shall be eternally thankful
for the whole experience.

By no means least is the fact that what
appeared to be disaster has been turned into a
wonderful door of opportunity for ministry.
Realizing that I could no longer undertake the
administration involved in the pastorate of such a
large church as Charlotte Chapel, my wife and I
were faced with a decision. Either we could take
a small pastorate which would involve less taxing
of strength, or believe that God had still a place
for me in the front line of battle in a wider
ministry.

We felt it right to choose the latter course, and
at the end of 1966, reluctantly, yet convinced
that I was in the will of God, I resigned from the
Chapel and from a localized ministry. Now,
visiting various mission fields each year,
preaching to missionaries and nationals in many
different countries, and experiencing the joy of
ministering the Word throughout the world, I
marvel at the wonderful ways of God. Truly He
has guided me with the skillfulness of His hands.

As I write, almost a decade has passed since

these events. I am learning it is always better
ahead with God, and one never graduates from
His school. Lessons learned have constantly to be
applied, and I would say with the Apostle, "I
don't mean to say I am perfect. I haven't learned
all I should even yet, but I keep working toward
that day when I will finally be all that Christ
saved me for and wants me to be . . . I strain to
reach the end of the race and receive the prize
for which God is calling us up to heaven because
of what Christ Jesus did for us" (Philippians
3:12–14). There is always the tendency to the
same failures which lead to further chastening
from heaven, but God abides faithful, as we
prove Him to be our Life and Sufficiency.

GEORGE BEVERLY SHEA, often called "America's Beloved Gospel Singer," was born in Winchester, Ontario. He has been singing the gospel around the globe for more than 30 years.

In 1938 Shea was offered a job as an announcer-singer at a Chicago station. Since

1944 he has been heard regularly on network radio. He has also recorded 49 sacred music albums.

Shea's network radio singing started on "Club Time," a program carried for over eight years on ABC and the Armed Forces networks as well as many independent stations. When Billy Graham, then pastor of the Village Church in Western Springs, Illinois, was taking over the "Songs in the Night" hymn program in 1943, he recalled hearing Shea's radio singing and enlisted him to help with the broadcast. That was the beginning of the long association between Graham and Shea. In 1947 the radio musician went to Graham's hometown of Charlotte, North Carolina, to sing in the first of Graham's city-wide crusades.

In 1949 the famous Los Angeles tent meeting catapulted Graham and his associates to national attention. From there, the Team went on to share the gospel on every inhabited continent. Because of Shea's weekly singing on the "Hour of Decision" broadcast (started in 1950) as well as his personal appearances, his voice is recognized now in Africa, Asia, Australia, Europe, and South America as well as in North America.

Shea and Cliff Barrows (the Team's choir director, platform emcee and radio-television program director) have been the nucleus of the Crusade musical team. They were joined by pianist Tedd Smith in 1950. Over the years, organists Don Hustad and John Innes have provided accompaniment.

The singer makes his home in Western Springs, Illinois. His wife Erma went to be with the Lord in September of 1976.

Rejected: Opportunity of a Lifetime
George Beverly Shea

It was the chance of a lifetime. The Fred Waring group of the thirties—the Lynn Murray singers—had a spot for me. I couldn't believe it. The realization of all my dreams. There was only one hitch that made it less than perfect, but let me backtrack a moment.

Born the son of a Wesleyan Methodist minister in Winchester, Ontario, Canada, I came to New York in 1928 when Dad accepted a call to Jersey City's First Wesleyan Methodist Church, just a stone's throw from Manhattan.

I went to work as a medical secretary at the Mutual Life Insurance Company and for nine years it was my livelihood. Before and after work, however, I spent my time engaged in my greatest love, singing. In the mornings many of those years, I sang on Jersey City radio station WKBO. The program was aired from seven to seven-thirty. How well I remember jumping out of bed at five-thirty, going over to the church and warming up the tonsils at the organ before taking a Bergen Avenue bus to the studio in time for the theme song.

After the program, I took the tube from Journal Square to the MONY offices on Nassau, near Wall Street. Following work, I usually had voice lessons or practiced alone. In addition to being a soloist at Dad's church, I sang occasionally at Calvary Baptist Church where my coach, Price Boone, was a featured soloist. Then too I filled in a bass part one night a week and every Sunday on Erling C. Olsen's popular program *Meditations in the Psalms* over Station WMCA.

All of this singing was done as an avocation. I was not a professional and doubted that I ever would be, for few people at that time were making a living in the religious music field and it looked as if I might spend my life in the insurance business. Not that this bothered me. I enjoyed the work and was quite happy to be able to sing a la carte. It was an opportunity to serve the Lord and I accepted my situation as His will for me at that time.

Some years earlier I had vowed to let God open the doors and not get in His way, impatiently running ahead trying every doorknob in sight. I reasoned, and still do, that if God had some new direction in mind He would speak to me about it—if I made it a point to listen. It is a principle I have employed throughout life.

Erma and I had been married a couple of years when the "turning point" opportunity came. I was making $34.50 a week.

It all began one spring day shortly before lunch. A singing pal of mine phoned the office, his voice full of excitement:

"Hey, Bev, did you hear that Lynn Murray is holding auditions this afternoon at CBS?"

I told him I hadn't heard.

"Well, I'm going to try out. Why not come along and sing something?"

I said I would think about it and possibly meet him there. The Lynn Murray Singers were one of the top groups of that day, and it was indeed a real opportunity.

"Is this something I should do, Lord?" I

prayed silently at my desk. Sensing no negative feelings, I decided to go to the audition. Fortunately, I had some music along so the only thing I had to do was to get off work early. That arranged, I hurried over to CBS.

Emerson Williams, another person who coached me, had advised me not long before to "sing the heart songs. . . ." "Swanee River" and "Down to the River" were a couple of warm numbers which I liked and considered in this category.

While nervously waiting my turn I learned that the job paid $75 a week, more than double what I was making. Furthermore, it offered national radio exposure on CBS. By the time my number came up, Mr. Murray had listened to about twenty singers and all of them had received polite attention, but not much more than a "Thank you. Next. . . ." A good many of them struck me as better bass baritones than myself. More than once my nerve weakened and I considered sneaking out a side door. But while I was searching for a convenient exit my name was called.

Though shaking like a leaf, once I got into the song, "Swanee River," I felt at ease. Mr. Murray got up out of his chair and, with face inscrutable, walked toward me. *He's going to give me a dressing down for wasting his time,* I thought. I was wrong.

He smiled and said: "I liked that. Do you have something else?"

At first his words didn't make an impression. Then they got through. He wanted an encore. "Well . . . y-y-yes," I stammered. I went to the briefcase and pulled out a rumpled version of "Down to the River," which was too high for my range but it had been transposed three notes lower. When I handed the scribbled-up version to the pianist he scratched and then shook his head. He couldn't read it.

While I was trying to explain what all the confusing directions meant, Mr. Murray, perhaps somewhat annoyed at the delay, came back and sat down at the piano himself. He knew the music and played it from memory. His knowledge of the song increased my confidence immensely and this time I did my best.

After I had finished the second "river" number, Mr. Murray nodded approvingly and handed me a piece of music ("Song of the Vagabonds" from Rudolph Friml's *The Vagabond King*), which they were going to sing at the Texas Centennial.

"I want you to learn this right away," Mr. Murray said. "We'll be in touch."

I took the music and wandered out of the studio in somewhat of a daze. I was about to become a member of the famous Lynn Murray Singers. That's what it meant. No question about it.

On my way home, I studied the libretto. Suddenly my eyes fell on a line which brought me up short. ". . . and to hell with Burgundy," it read. *Could I sing that line in good conscience?* I asked myself. Furthermore, the implications of performing in the secular world of show business gripped me for the first time. *Can one be a Christian and be a part of such things?* I pondered. As a boy, my mother and father taught me to take great care in expressing myself. *Hell* and *damn* and other commonly-heard expletives were not a part of our conversations.

That night I prayed about the dilemma. I thought of the hurt I might bring to Dad and the family. Alton was studying for the ministry and Whitney was teaching at Houghton College. I also thought about the radio and church singing and the disappointment my going into the secular field of music might bring to the people who had been helping me.

"God," I prayed, "I don't know why You have led me into this—maybe You're trying to test me. Anyway I'm not going to accept their offer if they make it. I can't think this is the way You'd have me serve You."

The next day Mr. Murray's secretary called and said, "Mr. Shea, congratulations. You are now one of the Lynn Murray Singers."

I swallowed hard and answered: "I thank you for the invitation, but have decided I won't be able to accept the job. Please thank Mr. Murray for me and tell him I appreciate his kind offer." They called back again trying to sell me on the idea, but I held firm even though greatly tempted.

The next few days were filled with torment. "What a fool you are, Bev," one voice inside would say. Then I'd hear, "You did the right thing, my son." Finally I put the thought to rest. I was positive I had done the right thing yet puzzled as to why God would require me to make such a tough choice.

My friend obtained the job instead and I was happy for him, because he wanted it more than anything else. However, I am not sure it was the best move for him either. It led to others like it and gradually he seemed to drift further and further away from the church. So it was a turning point for both of us.

As I look back on that day, I realize how important it was. For just a short time later a much different opportunity came my way.

Each summer I sang one week of my vacation at the Pinebrook Bible Conference in the

Pennsylvania Poconos and the summer following my decision on the Lynn Murray job was no exception.

The meetings opened on Sunday night, and I had the privilege of singing in a service in which Dr. Will Houghton spoke. (After serving as minister of Calvary Baptist Church in New York, Dr. Houghton had become the president of Moody Bible Institute in Chicago.)

The next day Erma and I were out walking when we heard someone call out, "Mr. Shea." It was Dr. Houghton, typically formal in greeting though warm at heart.

"Have you a minute?" he asked.

Erma excused herself and there, under those towering pines, we talked. I can still find the spot.

Dr. Houghton began, intently, "I've been thinking about you and I wonder—have you ever considered Christian radio as a vocation?"

"No, sir," I told him, "I haven't."

"Well, there is a staff opening this fall at WMBI (the Moody station in Chicago) that I think you could fill."

"You're very kind," I replied, "but my radio experience has been limited to singing. I'm no announcer nor much of a talker."

"I think you may be underestimating yourself," he smiled kindly. "Nevertheless, let me do some checking. I don't have any doubts about your ability. Let's correspond about it."

"I'd like that," I answered.

Erma and I returned to New York that weekend, and I went back to work at the insurance company the following Monday morning. For several days all of our spare moments were spent talking about the question Dr. Houghton had raised.

Erma seemed hesitant about going to Chicago.

In fact, she prayed that Dr. Houghton would not write.

"We're happy in New York, and you are receiving many opportunities to sing," she contended. "All of our relatives and friends are in the East, and we know practically no one in Chicago."

I quoted one of my favorite Scripture verses to her, one that I always turn to when faced with such a problem. "In everything you do, put God first, and he will direct you and crown your efforts with success" (Prov. 3:6).

Thursday night of that week I was late getting home because I had taken a voice lesson after work. As I entered the apartment, Erma came running out of the kitchen waving an envelope.

"It's from Dr. Houghton!" she said excitedly. "Open it. I've been dying to know what it says."

We went into the kitchen and sat down at the table. Dinner was ready, so I suggested we pray first.

"Lord, You know that we want most of all to do Your will. Whatever is in this letter, help us to make the right decision. The most important thing is that we honor You."

I opened the letter and read it partly aloud, partly to myself—giving Erma the key phrases. ". . . seriously interested in your joining us . . . need to know your approximate salary at present . . . what are you paying in rent . . . how soon could you come to Chicago if we can work out the details? . . . write as quickly as possible."

"*Chee*-cago, here we come," Erma said with a smirk.

"Not quite yet," I said. "There are lots of unresolved questions. But say the Lord does open the way? Would moving to Chicago make you all that unhappy?"

"I guess I'll just have to find another husband in New York," she teased. Then, she gave me a kiss and asked, "Should I get the suitcases out tonight or tomorrow?"

I wrote back immediately, answering Dr. Houghton's questions. My boss, Mr. Harold Voege, was wonderful about the offer.

"Bev," he exclaimed, "that's a tremendous opportunity. I'll pray for you."

Within a matter of days, we received another letter bearing a Moody Bible Institute return address. It contained an out-and-out invitation to sing every Sunday afternoon on Dr. Houghton's new program, *Let's Go Back to the Bible,* which was to be carried on a network of stations. If I accepted, I would be needed by September first. The WMBI staff position would not begin for six months. Meanwhile, I would be assigned to the school's promotion department.

Erma and I had set up some qualifications for our acceptance, a kind of "laying out the fleece," and all of them had been satisfied. That night I wrote Dr. Houghton:

"After much prayer and meditation, Erma and I feel led to accept. . . ."

When I told Mr. Voege, he congratulated me with tears in his eyes. "We will miss you, Bev," he said, "but I am sure the Lord's hand is in this."

A couple of weeks later the whole medical department, including twelve doctors, threw a going-away party for me. They presented me with a number of gifts, including a beautiful leather suitcase, which was really needed. A few days later it was filled with clothes and I said good-bye to New York.

Erma and I had decided it would be best if I went to Chicago first, spending a month or so getting oriented and settled before she joined me, and so near the end of August, 1938, I boarded a Chicago-bound train at Grand Central Station. Because there was a few dollars difference between coach and Pullman, I chose to spend the overnight trip sitting up.

My feelings as the train moved westward were ones of great expectation, yet not in my wildest dreams could I have imagined the scope of the spiritual adventure in store.

As shadows swept across the summer landscape hurrying by the window and night ended the show, I fell back in the seat full of questions about the tomorrows ahead. But I was also reflecting on the events that had led up to this move, especially the crossroad I passed a few months before—the opportunity to sing with the Lynn Murray group.

Now it all made sense. If I had not said "No" to that offer, it would have precluded the Chicago opportunity, and later meeting Billy Graham. I knew beyond any doubt—that God had an area of service He would bless. Many times since when I've faced difficult decisions, temptations that nearly swayed me, I remember how God had worked in that early experience.

I can still feel the great satisfaction that encompassed me on that train ride west. As sleep came on, I pulled my topcoat up tight around my shoulders, nestled down in the seat, and closed my eyes. An outer warmth came over me, matching an inner warmth—a harmony I felt with God.

Just before dozing off I uttered the shortest prayer I think I've ever said. It was simply, "Thank You, Lord."

DR. CLYDE W. TAYLOR served
evangelical interests in Washington, D.C., from
1944 until his retirement at the end of 1974. He
has served as secretary of public affairs and
general director of the National Association of
Evangelicals and executive secretary of the
Evangelical Foreign Missions Association.

Prior to coming to Washington, Dr. Taylor served as a missionary of the Christian and Missionary Alliance in Peru and later in Colombia where he established a Bible institute. He was a pastor in metropolitan Boston and taught at Gordon College.

Active in the organization of the World Evangelical Fellowship in 1951, Dr. Taylor was elected International Secretary of the WEF in August 1971 and currently is continuing in that position during the transfer of responsibility to his successor.

Dr. Taylor has served as chairman of the executive committee, World Congress on Evangelism (Berlin, 1966); a member of the Executive Committee, U.S. Congress on Evangelism (Minneapolis, 1969); co-chairman, Latin American Congress on Evangelism (Bogota, Colombia, 1969), and Executive Planning Committee member of the International Congress on World Evangelization (Lausanne, Switzerland, 1974).

Dr. Taylor was also coordinator of the Consultation on Saturation Evangelism held in Switzerland in September 1969. He is a member of the Board of the American Bible Society, and is listed in *Who's Who in America.*

He is married to the former Ruth Marstaller of Durham, Maine. They have one son and three daughters. Dr. Taylor continues his residence in Washington, D.C.

Educated at Nyack Missionary Training Institute, Gordon College, and Boston University, Dr. Taylor received honorary degrees from Western Baptist Theological Seminary, Houghton College, and Malone College.

Tapping God's Resources
Clyde W. Taylor

When I was six my parents were saved. After
that time we attended a fine evangelical church
but I held off accepting Christ even though I was
brought up in the church. I became a Christian
when I was a high school freshman in Phoenix,
Arizona.

My father was a contractor and builder so I
spent many hours hanging around buildings
under construction. My father helped to get me a
summer job as an apprentice in carpentry the first
vacation from high school. However, I already
had plans for my life—and they did not include
carpentry. I would be a mining engineer. But
such early feelings failed to consider the spiritual.

Our church was a missionary-minded center
and frequent missionary speakers appeared. Even
after accepting Christ, however, I had no
inclination to be a missionary or to enter the
ministry. I did take an active part in Sunday
school and youth meetings, and of course we had
family worship every night. But I really hadn't
asked the Lord about His plans for my life.

During the summer of 1920, after my second
year in high school, I worked with a crew of
carpenters. We made heavy wooden trusses forty
feet long to hold up the roof of a warehouse. As
we finished each truss another crew of men
would pick it up, carry it to one side, and stand
it against a side wall. Fearing that the whole
stack, standing straight up, might topple over, the
foreman pulled me off the crew. He told me to

lean against the stack to make sure they didn't fall.

All went well until one of the handlers carrying the next truss tripped. That threw the rest of the men off balance. Instead of stopping just before lowering the truss to give me time to get out of the way, they pitched forward. The truss fell across my legs at the knees, rupturing the joints. They caught it before it completely broke my legs.

Doctors seemed able to do little in those days. My parents took me to several specialists but they didn't want to operate. Soon the knee joints became dry and the knees greatly enlarged. It was very painful to bend them, to walk normally, or even to stand after sitting for some time. That fall in high school I dropped out of ROTC and all sports. The knees pained me most of the time. Now I was compelled to think again of my future and what I could do with my knees getting worse, and me a cripple.

In my junior year at high school, our pastor started a Sunday morning series of sermons on the book of James. When he preached on the final half of the fifth chapter, my attention was caught by verses 14 and 15: "Is anyone sick? He should call for the elders of the church and they should pray over him and pour a little oil upon him, calling on the Lord to heal him. And their prayer, if offered in faith, will heal him, for the Lord will make him well; and if his sickness was caused by some sin, the Lord will forgive him." His topic for the exposition was "Prayer and the Forgiveness of Sins." I waited in vain for him to speak on the two specific verses. The sermon ended and I wondered why he skipped them. I spoke to my mother about it. She suggested I go forward after the benediction and ask him.

The pastor smiled at me when I asked him. He wanted to know why I was so interested in those verses. I reminded him that I had a pair of damaged knees. I asked him if he believed those verses were to be taken literally because I had never seen anyone anointed and prayed for in the church (this was not a ministry that the church practiced). He said he believed they should be taken literally and then asked me if I believed God would heal my legs. I replied that if the verses meant what they said, I would certainly like to do what they instructed one to do.

The pastor saw one of his daughters standing nearby. He asked her to go out front and see if any of the deacons might still be there. She soon returned with five of them. He then sent her next door to the parsonage for a bottle of olive oil. Asking the deacons to be seated on the front row beside me, he explained our conversation. Then he reread the passage to us and suggested we all pray in turn. This we did. Then the pastor asked me if I knew of any unforgiven sin in my life. I didn't. He suggested that I kneel—a real problem and painful, but I did it. He then took the bottle of oil and asked the deacons to lay their hands on me.

"Lord Jesus," he prayed, "we believe this command in Thy Word by the Apostle James and we are doing just as You told us. I now anoint Clyde with oil and we ask You, Lord, that You heal his knees."

Instantly I felt as if a slight electric shock went through my body. When the pastor asked me to stand I was aware that the pain was gone. In starting to stand, I rocked back on my heels, something I hadn't been able to do. Later when we examined the knees we noted they had shrunk back to normal size. Curiously, one thing wasn't restored: the reflexes in both knees. Even now I have a hard time convincing doctors how I lost my reflexes.

Something far more important than the healing had taken place. I had a new relationship with the Lord. I had been involved in a step of faith that had made it possible for the Lord to manifest His power in my body. Prayer became real conversation with God. The spiritual implications of the healing made it necessary for me to rethink the relationship of God's will for my life in contrast to my plans.

As a direct result of the healing, I received a confidence in the promises of the Word that I had never known before. This has had a constant bearing on my life and decisions. In later years I have been shown promises in the Word by the Holy Spirit on which I have based decisions and action in the work of the church. Sometimes these have been criticized and opposed, but the Lord has stood back of His Word and vindicated our decisions and actions. On the other hand, I am aware of failing at times to take the Lord at His Word and as a result have not received His blessing.

About the time I was healed, the pastor had urged the prayer meeting crowd to memorize Romans 12. As the members memorized it, we would repeat the chapter in prayer meeting. During this repetition the Spirit began to bring to my mind the first two verses, "And so, dear brothers, I plead with you to give your bodies to God. Let them be a living sacrifice, holy—the kind he can accept. When you think of what he has done for you, is this too much to ask? Don't copy the behavior and customs of this world, but be a new and different person with a fresh newness in all you do and think. Then you will learn from your own experience how his ways will really satisfy you."

The Holy Spirit applied it to my life at that crisis time. I had no quarrel with the first verse. And I found that total surrender to Christ took me to the second verse and to God's will for my life. The spiritual impact of the healing and its resultant real relationship with Christ gradually overwhelmed me with the desire to do what He wanted me to do.

The Lord used the events in the church program to direct my thinking. At the next missionary conference I went forward to publicly indicate my willingness to go to the mission field if the Lord wanted me. I was increasingly impressed in my thinking that this was what He wanted. This seeking of His will for my life set a pattern for my decisions. The careful choice of a Bible school for training for missions took me to Nyack (N.Y.) Missionary Training Institute (now Nyack College) and also resulted in the channel for me to be sent out to the mission field: the Christian and Missionary Alliance.

As I look back these many years I can see God's hand permitting the accident in order to halt my stubborn determination to plan my own life. He used the physical trial to provide a means of demonstrating His power in my body. I still had many lessons to learn regarding the revealing of His will in my life and I have come to recognize several facts regarding this.

First, I found that my natural desires and decisions for my life were not necessarily God's plans for me. As I finished Bible school I volunteered for service in Africa. The mission said they needed me to form part of a four-man team for pioneer work in the Peruvian jungle.

After much prayer I took it as the hand of the Lord using others to lead me. I went to Peru. After furlough, including more college training and marriage, I wanted to go back to Peru but the Lord pointed me to Colombia. In every decision I have been called to make with regard to the Lord's will, it seemed I preferred something else but eventually came to see God's leading and obeyed.

The second fact that bothered me was in the application of Romans 11:29 to my life (I had run across this verse while studying the context of the passage in Chapter 12). "For God's gifts and his call can never be withdrawn; he will never go back on his promises." Since God called me to missionary work, why did He keep me home and take me into the pastorate and then to serve evangelicals in Washington? Eventually I came to see that God didn't change His calling. He hadn't called me to Peru, to Colombia, and to a pastorate in Quincy, Massachusetts. He called me to a service. This calling does not change. But God didn't *call* me to a place. He *sent* me. Then in His divine strategy, he *moved* me. The recognition of this fact answered a question that had bothered me for years.

A third fact became a dominant force in my life: the fear of getting out of God's will. Many offers to change my place of service, perhaps to improve my financial or social conditions, have presented themselves during the last quarter of a century. I have developed a standard answer to such offers. I thank them and then state frankly that I am afraid to move as long as I have the assurance that I am still in God's will. I do believe there must be a willingness to change if God is leading, but we have found that God's will is good—it becomes acceptable, enjoyable and it provides a mature security to know *where* God wants you, *when* He wants you, doing *what* He wants you to do. When that happens the Lord becomes responsible for the results. He sees to it that His purpose is carried out.

This incident of healing, after my salvation, was the big event that directed my life to one of service for the Lord. In many ways it laid the basis on which the Holy Spirit taught me the power of the prayer of faith. The authority of the Bible and especially the promises were demonstrated to me as effective means of tapping the resources that God has made available for us. The surrender of my will to God for His direction and orders never lessened my responsibility to exercise the will to obey Him.

While I was still in high school, Psalm 37:5 became my life verse as I learned the importance of surrender to Christ. "Commit everything you do to the Lord. Trust him to help you do it and he will." Commitment of my life to the Lord and the exercise of trust in Him has brought into my life opportunities and responsibilities that I never would have known had not the Lord used an accident to redirect my life.

DR. KENNETH N. TAYLOR is the
founder and president of Tyndale House
Publishers in Wheaton (Carol Stream), Illinois.
   A 1938 graduate of Wheaton College, Dr.
Taylor also studied at Dallas Theological
Seminary and Northern Baptist Theological
Seminary. He has received honorary degrees

from Wheaton College, Trinity Evangelical Divinity School, and Huntington College.

Best known for his Living Bible paraphrase, Dr. Taylor has authored many other books, including *Is Christianity Credible?, Stories for the Children's Hour, Devotions for the Children's Hour, The Bible in Pictures for Little Eyes,* and *Taylor's Bible Story Book.*

Dr. Taylor was 1974 recipient of the Distinguished Public Service award given by Messiah College and the Better World Award presented by the National VFW Auxiliary.

In 1973, he received the Distinguished Service Citation from the International Society of Christian Endeavor and the Nelson Bible Award from Thomas Nelson, Inc.

Religious Heritage of America presented him a special award in 1972, and Layman's National Bible Committee honored him with a citation in 1971.

Dr. Taylor also is publisher of *The Christian Reader, Have a Good Day, The Church Around the World* and *Bookshorts.*

He is a director of Short Terms Abroad, president of Tyndale House Foundation, president of Living Bibles International, international president of Kingsway Publications Ltd., Eastbourne, England, member of the board of directors of Interskrift Forlage Aktiebolag, Sweden, and trustee of Fuller Theological Seminary.

Dr. Taylor and his wife, the former Margaret Louise West, have ten children.

I Suffered with Borden of Yale

Kenneth N. Taylor

My most important encounter with God, as I
remember, occurred when I was home in
Portland, Oregon, (nearer Beaverton, actually,
but it was hardly on the map in those days) after
my sophomore year at Wheaton College. Equally
important things no doubt have happened, but
were less dramatic and less remembered.

I had been facing enormous emotional
problems at school that year, mostly about girls.
One in particular I had known for several years
and didn't know whether to go ahead and try to
get engaged or to forget the whole thing. Either
way seemed impossible, hence the emotional
trauma.

As a result I had become very depressed and
my relationship to God was quite unsatisfactory.
An overwhelming desire for acceptance,
popularity, campus leadership, planning for
prestige and wealth in the future—these had
begun to wipe out my desire for God.
Consequently the Spirit of God and the spirit of
the flesh were striving mightily within me. Here
again my emotional interior was in complete
disharmony and disarray.

For some reason I was not out baling hay on
that particular afternoon. I had decided to read a
book I had heard about called *Borden of Yale*. I
found it fascinating. It was the biography of a
student at Yale University. He had all the good
things I was striving for: popularity, wealth (his
father was a millionaire and had apparently

bequeathed most of it to Bill), he was on
important Boards of Directors of large Christian
institutions even at his young age. Yet his daily
times with God were regular and effective in his
Bible study and prayer.

To my horror, as I read on, I discovered that
he was planning to become a missionary! This
was the farthest from my dreams and cut across
all my delightful fantasies for the future. Utterly
fascinated by this time, I read on.

Sure enough, soon after graduation Bill
Borden headed for Cairo, Egypt, to begin
spending his life in the almost untouched Muslim
world of the Mideast (in those days they were
called Mohammedans or Moslems). Well, I really
had to admire the man. Of course I began to feel
terribly uneasy as I thought of my own selfish
desires for the very things he was happily giving
up for God. Should I follow the example of this
man I had learned to admire so much, and give
up all (which I didn't yet have) and follow my
Lord in whatever directions He might give to
me? I wondered.

But then came the shock of my young life as I
read on in this disturbing book. Within a couple
of weeks after Bill arrived on the mission field
he became ill. Excited about the miracle about to
occur in his healing, I continued to read. But it
didn't happen.

He died.

And my new spiritual world collapsed. I laid
the book aside, bitter at God. So this is the way
He treated His most devoted servants and
lovers? And He expected *me* to follow Him after
seeing this demonstration of the way He treated
His people? Unbelieving, I stared at the floor
and let the full revulsion control me.

At that very moment, something happened I

cannot explain. In the midst of my revolting, I found myself down on my knees beside the chair where I had been reading. I was saying to God, "You always know what You are doing. I want to give my life to You like Bill Borden gave his, whether it means life or death. You tell me what to do and I'll do it."

From that time on, a dramatic turning point, my life progressively became quieter and stronger and ever more determined to follow God.

MAJOR W. IAN THOMAS was born in London and converted at the age of 12. He was in the Royal Fusiliers, an Infantry regiment, having been first commissioned in 1933.

Recalled from the Reserve, he served in the British Expeditionary Forces in France and Belgium at the outset of World War II and took part in the evacuation of Dunkirk. He also saw action in North Africa, Italy, and Greece.

Major Thomas is founder and director of the Capernwray Missionary Fellowship of Torchbearers, established in 1947 with international headquarters in Capernwray Hall, England. The organization has two centers each in Germany and Austria, one each in Spain, Sweden, Switzerland, France, New Zealand, Fiji, Australia, and Canada, and three centers in the United States: in California, Colorado and Texas, with administrative headquarters in Orlando, Florida.

Major Thomas, D.S.O., T.D., has ministered in the British Isles, most countries of Western Europe, Canada, United States, Australia, New Zealand, New Guinea, Singapore, Formosa, Japan, India, Pakistan, many countries of Africa, West Indies, and most countries of South America.

The Day I Quit
W. Ian Thomas

"What do you think we are, cannibals?"

That, in all probability, would have been the response of my family to anybody who had suggested we were not Christians!

Born in England, white-skinned, comfortably middle-class, and respectable members in good standing of a local church congregation—what more could reasonably have been expected of us?

There was nothing exaggerated or lop-sided, mind you, about our practice of religion. We were "once-ers." To go to church on Sunday morning (wind and weather permitting) was respectable, but to have gone twice would have been fanatical. As a child I was given a Bible, though nobody for one moment imagined that I would want to read it, let alone be seen doing so. That really would have been in bad taste. I could find the appropriate place in the Prayer Book, but later, once my interest had been sufficiently aroused to look, I tried to find John's Gospel in the Old Testament.

"Christianized"—but pathetically less than Christian. Bearing only that thin veneer of churchmanship which passes muster in a wayward, godless society for true religion—a society in which songs are still sung with fervor about the "faith of our Fathers," but in which men and women neither know their God nor the inspiration of their faith.

In spite of this, even before I reached my teens there was an unspoken quest and an indefinable urge within my heart—a longing after God. I can remember talking to Him about the trivial things which mean so much and loom so large in the little world of a small boy. But my words echoed into space. God was "somewhere out there," but I didn't know where to find Him. He was out of sight, beyond my reach, and in a realm of unreality. I didn't know how to get His attention.

It was a boy much my own age who provided the link. Kenneth, at thirteen, was a few months older than I. He had found a good thing. As my friend he wanted to share his discovery with me.

Never having been to Sunday school in my life, I found it somewhat of a novelty to go with him to a Boys' Bible Class on a Sunday afternoon. It was one of some three hundred such classes organized by the Crusaders' Union throughout the British Isles. Interdenominational it was, solidly based on the Bible as the Word of God and faithfully proclaiming salvation through faith in Jesus Christ alone, who died and rose again for our justification.

The atmosphere was friendly and distinctly cheerful; the Bible seemed familiar and meaningful to those who, unapologetically, held it in their hands and taught its message. Those who spoke and prayed did so with assurance and conviction. I was left in no doubt: they knew the One of whom and to whom they were speaking. I was fascinated by such a firsthand knowledge of God.

It was not to get converted, however, that I accompanied my young friend, Kenneth, on his second visit to that summer camp. One year before he had received Christ into his life there. The simple fact was that I didn't know what it meant to be converted. This was an entirely new language to me, to which I had not previously been exposed. Conversion, redemption—the idea that I could be "saved" through receiving Christ personally as my Savior, because He had died in my place upon the Cross, that I could be "born again," possessing "eternal life"—to all of this I was a total stranger.

Everything seemed natural and obvious to those who led that Crusader Camp, to those whom I had met in the Bible class, and to the friendly young men who organized the games and took us swimming. Surprisingly enough, to many of the youngsters, too, who participated with me in these activities, Jesus Christ was alive and real and the obvious object of their love and loyalty.

I didn't find it difficult to listen to the camp chaplain, Mr. Lawrence Head, as he spoke to us in the large canvas marquee (tent with open sides). For one thing, he frothed at the mouth when he spoke and for that reason was affectionately known as "Bubbly Head." It was fun watching the bubbles, wondering on which side of his mouth they would burst first! Mr. Head was not a professional preacher, but a businessman who had a lovely way of communicating the truth of the gospel in such a way that youngsters such as I then was could understand.

On the third night of that camp, I heard from the tenth chapter of John's Gospel about the Good Shepherd who laid down His life for the sheep. I understood clearly that Christ had died in my place so that I might be forgiven. If only I would ask Him, in simple, childlike faith, He would come into my life as my Savior and I would receive eternal life. I understood that from that moment, forgiven, I would become a child of God and never perish, for He would never leave nor forsake me.

There was no open invitation to respond nor
aftermeeting for instruction, just a quiet moment
at the end of the meeting during which any boy
in his heart could speak to the Lord Jesus Christ,
thankfully claim forgiveness through His shed
blood, and receive Him as his Savior.

I told nobody then what had happened in my
heart, but on that evening of my third day in
camp, life for me began in an entirely new
dimension. There were to be consequences far
beyond my wildest dreams, calculated completely
to change the course of my future years. I had
been redeemed!

That, however, was not my most significant
encounter with God. I had entered consciously
into the good of what Christ had done through
His atoning death, in reconciling me to God. I
had not come to understand the purpose for
which that reconciliation had been effected, nor
the solid substance of that spiritual regeneration
which in consequence had taken place, though
still unknown to me, by the coming of the Holy
Spirit to live within my human spirit.

To have testified then, as I did, that "Christ
lived in my heart" was simply another way of
saying that I had been converted, that Christ was
my Savior, that my sins had been forgiven and
that I was on my way to Heaven. That Jesus
Christ as my God and Creator had actually taken
up residence through His Holy Spirit within His
creature, to share His life with me on earth, was
something the significance of which had not as
yet begun to dawn upon my soul. I just didn't
know how wealthy I had become.

"Jesus living in my heart" was not an
unmeaningful expression in terms of my
redemption. It represented more a sentimental
attachment, a sense of gratitude or term of

endearment rather than a working relationship between man and God in spiritual union. My gratitude to Christ for dying in my place motivated me with genuine sincerity to work *for* Him and to represent His cause, but He remained external to my endeavors. As the honored *object* only of those activities, Christ still seemed to me so very, very far away in Heaven. He had not as yet become the active *origin* of those activities, resident here on earth within my soul.

Though without encouragement in my own home, I took real delight in reading my Bible and enjoyed the company best of those who loved my Savior. I shall never cease to be thankful to God for those who offered me their friendship and their counsel during those formative years of my early Christian life. Bible class and camp remained the main source of instruction and inspiration and later, quite naturally, the main area of Christian activity.

At the age of fifteen I assumed the leadership of the Christian group at my high school, with a prayer meeting each morning before commencement, an evangelistic meeting each Monday lunch hour and a Bible study Thursday afternoons. It was at that age, too, that I first dedicated my life to missionary service with my eyes on Africa. I began preaching in the open air on Hampstead Heath, a public park in the vicinity of my home in London, England.

Convinced that I would be more useful on the mission field in Africa as a doctor, on graduating from high school at the age of seventeen, through the generosity of my parents, I enrolled at London University to study medicine. Already by then an assistant leader in the Crusader Bible Class through which I had been converted, I assumed additional responsibilities in the Inter-Varsity Christian Union at St. Bartholomew's Hospital where I was studying.

At the same time I established a Christian club for underprivileged boys in the heart of the city. My vacations, summer and winter, were now wholly dedicated to evangelistic crusades, Bible camps, Christian sailing cruises, seaside missions, and other forms of missionary outreach. In my zeal I had joined the rat-race.

I began to feel like the Mississippi steamboat that stopped every time it blew its whistle. There was enough steam to make a noise, but not enough power to drive the pistons. I could "rev" the engine and be impressive, but somehow I couldn't get the power from under the hood into the wheels on the road. I wanted to shift gears but couldn't find the gear-shift; that can be frustrating!

It was not that I differed from the rest, for I saw no evidence in others that any better quality of life could be expected. The things that I did in Christian service and the way I did them, I had learned from those who had done the same before me. All conformed to pattern and appeared entirely acceptable in the light of precedent and common practice. We all ran by the same rules, but for me the race was nearly over. I was a very, very tired rat!

In spite of my noblest endeavors, I was baffled at my inability to bring others to the point of accepting Christ as their Savior. Nor was there any evidence that the words on my lips were actually being translated into the reality of other people's lives, though most earnestly expressed. I finally lost all expectation that this could ever be.

Coupled with this increasing sense of futility in all that I attempted to do was the increasing consciousness of personal failure and defeat in my sincere desire to honor Christ by reflecting His likeness in my life. All this brought me to despair. I knew I would be as useless in Africa as I had been in England, for crossing an ocean would not make me a saint. Nor could carving my way through the scrub with a bush-knife in one hand and a Bible in the other turn a spiritual pygmy into a spiritual giant! I wanted so much to be a man of God, but I was desperately tired and very, very discouraged.

No words could have been more applicable to my case than those of God to His people through the lips of His servant in the prophecy of Haggai, Chapter 1, Verse 6: "You plant much but harvest little. You have scarcely enough to eat or drink, and not enough clothes to keep you warm. Your income disappears, as though you were putting it into pockets filled with holes!"

The conditions that then prevailed in Judah bore painful testimony to the sorry state of my own soul.

The scanty harvest scarcely justified the effort made in sowing the seed. In my life were rampant signs of spiritual undernourishment. I came to drink but went away thirsty, shivering in the threadbare promises of better times which never came. My spiritual income was swallowed up by the high cost of living in a troubled, sin-sick society, where the demands made upon me always outmatched my spiritual output.

God said to Judah then: "Consider your ways", and on my knees one night, in tears of helplessness, I considered mine!

What a relief it is to discover that you have never been a greater failure than God always expected you to be. I unburdened my soul to a loving, understanding Savior.

The perfect friend is one who knows the worst
    about you,
And loves you just the same.
There's only One Who loves like that,
And Jesus is His name.

I told Him how utterly discouraged I had
become. I could look back only upon seven years
of barrenness; any further effort now seemed
futile.

God knows, I thought to myself, *how hard I have
tried—desperately hard, and yet all to no avail.* All
hope within my heart had been abandoned.
Noble longings and strivings after godliness had
withered at the roots. In deep despair I prayed:
"Lord Jesus, I love You with all my heart and I
shall never cease to be thankful that You died
upon the Cross for me. I know that You are my
Redeemer. I know that my sins are forgiven. I
know that I am on my way to Heaven. I know
that I have cherished only one ambition—to be
used in Your service to bring others to Yourself
and to bring glory to Your Name. But I am
beaten. I just don't have what it takes, and I am
on my back. I'm sorry, but I quit!"

I thought the Lord Jesus Christ would be
greatly disappointed, but I almost heard Him
sigh with relief. It was as though He said to me
then: "Thank you! I have been waiting for this
for seven years. All that time, with great sincerity
but with misguided dedication, you have been
trying to live *for* me a life that only I can live
through you. *At last I am in business!*"

Yes, indeed He was! He was in business—the
glorious business of demonstrating the
overwhelming adequacy of an indwelling Savior
to meet every last need of those who will let
Him be God in the man, and who will give Him

the opportunity of proving that He is big enough for the job.

In a moment of revelation I graduated out of bankruptcy. Out of the bitterness of despair I discovered my true wealth—that "treasure" which God, as the seal of our redemption, is pleased to place within the earthen vessels of our frail humanity. Christ Himself—that "everyone can see that the glorious power within must be from God and is not our own" (2 Cor. 4:7).

I did not receive one thing more, at that moment, than had already been mine throughout the whole seven years of my previous Christian life—Christ Himself. I simply discovered that the spiritual poverty in which for so long I had been living stemmed from my ignorance of the true content of the Christian life. It was a poverty I had imposed upon myself in failing to appropriate the resources which I had so long possessed.

> *And since, when we were his enemies, we were brought back to God by the death of His Son, what blessings he must have for us now that we are his friends, and he is living within us! (Rom. 5:10).*

I had long been reconciled to God by the death of the Lord Jesus, but had wholly failed to grasp the fact that His death for me, in reconciling me to God, was designed to put His life in me so that I might be "saved by His life," deriving from Him every moment of every day the divine dynamic which makes life essentially miraculous.

"For to me, living means opportunities for Christ" (Phil. 1:21).

"I have been crucified with Christ: and I myself no longer live, but Christ lives in me . . ." (Gal. 2:20).

"And when Christ who is our real life comes back again, you will shine with him and share in all his glories" (Col. 3:4).

"He died for us so that we can live with him forever, whether we are dead or alive at the time of his return" (1 Thess. 5:10).

These were the familiar Scriptures which suddenly leapt into life as my soul was flooded with light. My spirit was released. I experienced a profound sense of peace and quiet confidence. My heart overflowed with an unspeakable joy.

Jesus Christ Himself, alive, and living in me!

Not gazing distantly through the clouds, but sharing His life with me on earth on the way to Heaven and able to release through me all His illimitable resources in every new situation.

How long and how wearily I had hoped, begged, and prayed for what was already mine—and I mean all of it! At last I could see it. All that He was, I had. I could not have more and needed never to enjoy less. Simply take, and say "Thank You!"

Born inhabited and governed by an old Adam nature hostile to God and not subject to His laws, at my new birth, according to His great and precious promises, I had become "partaker of the divine nature" (2 Peter 1:4). It was now open to me to walk either after the flesh or after the Spirit, to be governed by the old nature or by the new. That new nature, through the indwelling of the Holy Spirit, was the Divine nature: Christ Himself.

I realized then, for the first time, that in asking God to give me strength I had been asking God for strength either for that old, wicked Adam nature or else for Christ Himself, that new, sinless, Divine nature. To improve the former, God would give neither strength nor encouragement, for ". . . in my flesh dwells no good thing" (Rom. 7:18). The flesh would not get it, and of course Christ did not need it. So in asking, whose time had I been wasting? Both His and mine.

How gloriously simple! Christ does not *give* me strength, He *is* my strength. He does not *give* me victory, He *is* my victory. All that I could ever need at any time in any circumstance.

> *For it is from God alone that you have your life through Christ Jesus. He showed us God's plan of salvation; he was the one who made us acceptable to God; he made us pure and holy and gave himself to purchase our salvation. As it says in the Scriptures, "If anyone is going to boast, let him boast only of what the Lord has done" (1 Cor. 1:30, 31).*

That, without a doubt, was my most memorable encounter with God. I had learned to relate every new situation into which every new step took me to the Person of the Lord Jesus Christ Whose life I shared. He waited only for my availability to demonstrate His marvelous all-sufficiency.

I got up from my knees that evening to begin the adventure of letting Jesus Christ be God in the man, as once as Man He had allowed the Father to be God in Him. Within five weeks He had taken me out of medical school and launched me into that ministry which since then has taken me into every part of the world. Nothing has changed the principle, but I never cease to be amazed at the sheer wonder of it. Every day becomes more exciting in the growing experience of discovering just how great God is.

This is my testimony, for it is the story of my life. I have not told you of some special blessing reserved for the few and least of all for those who are worthy. This is the privilege that none of us deserve, but the undeserved birthright of all who claim redemption through His blood and, indwelt by His Spirit, are born of God. You share the life of Jesus Christ on earth!

To share the life of Jesus Christ is to live miraculously. Why settle for less?

> *Now I have given up everything else—I have found it to be the only way to really know Christ and to experience the mighty power that brought him back to life again, and to find out what it means to suffer and to die with him. So, whatever it takes, I will be one who lives in the fresh newness of life of those who are alive from the dead (Phil. 3:10, 11).*

> *For I can do everything God asks me to with the help of Christ who gives me the strength and power (Phil. 4:13).*

DR. LARRY WARD, president of Food for the Hungry, Inc., travels throughout the world many months each year. He has logged millions of air miles in repeated visits to more than 60 countries.

Before assuming his present responsibilities, he was vice president/overseas director of World

Vision International. Previously he served as managing editor of *Christianity Today* and *Christian Life* magazines, and was for eight years executive secretary of the Evangelical Press Association and director of its worldwide E. P. News Service.

Dr. Ward is a graduate of Wheaton College. Yonsei University of Seoul, Korea, and Azusa Pacific College have awarded him doctor's degrees in the fields of Laws and Humanities. He was honored by the Republic of Korea in 1969, and the government of South Vietnam bestowed on him its highest decoration in the last hours before the collapse of that country in April 1975.

According to the *Los Angeles Herald Examiner,* Dr. Ward "has probably looked into more hungry faces than any other man of our day."

His non-sectarian relief agency, Food for the Hungry, was organized in January 1971 as a non-profit, charitable organization.

"This Poor Man Cried..."
Larry Ward

For the past five years, as I write these words, I have walked a road called "miracle."

I know that's an overworked word: miracle.

I realize someone might misunderstand, and try to read a note of spiritual pride into my simple statement.

So let me try to explain, and preface my explanation with this verse which to me sums it all up: "This poor man cried to the Lord—and the Lord heard him, and saved him out of his troubles" (Ps. 34:6).

Bangladesh, 1972: I had come here to Dacca in the will of God. Somehow, standing here in the battered airport which showed the ravages of war, I *knew* that.

Even before I had left my home in California to rush here, only hours after Bangladesh had been born as the newest (and eighth largest) nation in all the world, God had communicated to my heart the deep conviction that He Himself was perfectly timing this trip.

So here I stood—scared to death. All alone. Empty-handed. Ready to run.

No, I really hadn't forgotten that sense of His timing—that feeling that I would see the incredible synchronization of His purposes.

But I knew that three million people had died here. Ten million who had walked a trail of tears to India were now coming home—in rags and poverty, many of them to find that not only had their homes been destroyed, but even their villages had been completely obliterated—wiped off the face of the earth, with tall grass covering all traces of previous habitation.

And I knew also that an additional twenty million others here could also be classed as refugees, displaced within their own countries.

I was just one person. One empty-handed individual, bewildered and all alone in a strange country. I didn't know anyone; didn't know what to do or where to start.

So (to my shame, I admit it now), I looked at my watch. Despite that whisper of the Holy Spirit I had heard at home, that sense of divine timing which had seemed so unmistakable, I thought: *Well, nothing I can do here. Might as well catch the plane back to Calcutta. This is too big for me.*

Four hours later I was sipping tea there in Dacca in the house of the new President of Bangladesh.

Two days later a major plan had crystallized, and *incredible* contacts had developed which would eventually make that plan possible. The concept called for a massive food airlift within this ravaged country—and, thanks to those initial contacts, it later became a reality of compassion which saw over twenty million pounds of food carried to the stranded millions inside this context of heartbreak which was the new country of Bangladesh.

What happened after I stood there in the airport in near-panic? Some great new sense of revelation, some noble flash of inspiration, some daring plan?

No, I had simply prayed—and then remembered that I *did* know someone in Bangladesh. A missionary named Calvin Olson. I had heard that he and his wife, Marion, had voluntarily stayed on in Dacca through the previous nine months of dreadful war. God had preserved their lives, but they had recently been robbed at gun-and-dagger-point.

Even though there's nothing else I can do, I thought, *I can check at least on that one couple. Maybe I can help them a little. And then leave for Calcutta.*

But God had other plans. It seems that Cal Olson had a landlord he wanted me to meet—a man who twenty-four hours before had been named the first President of Bangladesh. And the President had concerns to share, contacts to suggest which eventually opened the door for one of the biggest relief efforts of all time.

Just coincidence?

A year later, there was *Nicaragua, 1972–3.* Our little plane had just landed in the pitch-black darkness of Managua. We knew that some 8,000 to 12,000 people had died here in the massive earthquake three or four days before; some 365,000 had been rendered suddenly homeless in a few seconds of midnight terror.

Beyond that we knew little else. The news reports had been fragmentary, and this was a new country to me. The only name I knew in all Nicaragua was that of General Somoza, the President—and it was a cinch he had never heard of me!

So now our four-man disaster relief team trudged across the darkened runway, and prayed as we did so. Headwinds had delayed us; apparently now we would have to wait all night before starting out to look for whomever God wanted us to meet and whatever it was He wanted us to do.

A needle in a haystack? We didn't even know what kind of "needle" we were looking for—and the earthquake had turned the "haystack" into a confusing shambles.

Then, out of the darkness, a kind young voice in warm welcome . . . a whistle . . . and a bus which mysteriously appeared.

"You've been very kind," I said to our young greeter. "What is your name?"

"Luis," he answered. "Luis *Somoza.*"

Fifteen minutes later that bus the President's nephew had arranged dropped us off—at the President's house! (It seems they didn't know where else to take us. Those headwinds and that resultant delay had been a blessing.)

And out of those first hours, as we met President Somoza and his extraordinary wife, and saw their remarkable dedication and around-the-clock effort to help their people, came the contacts and procedures which enabled us to later ship in over a half-million pounds of food, all of it placed in dedicated Christian hands for honest person-to-person distribution.

We had found that "needle" we were looking for—the most effective way in which to work—in the "haystack" which proved to be the Presidential Palace, the nerve center of the relief effort.

All this because of some ability of ours? Only if you mean *availability.* We made ourselves available, and God did the rest.

You see, "This poor man cried—and the Lord heard him, and saved him out of his troubles."

Still sound like coincidence?

A few months later, it was *Africa, 1973.* Time and space won't permit the whole recital, so I merely list:

1. My call to a travel agent booking a trip to West Africa (another area I did not know). "Pearl," I instructed, "I want several days in

Mauritania. I have never been there, don't know anyone, don't really know the situation. But a terrible drought reaches all across Africa south of the Sahara Desert. Looking at the map, I figure Mauritania must be one of the hardest-hit places."

2. A few hours later, that same day, a phone call from Washington, D.C.—a message from the office of Doug Coe of the international prayer breakfast movement. "Doug just called from Romania. He has been in Africa—wants to know if you have any plans to be there. He especially wants to urge you to go to *Mauritania*."

3. Three weeks later, I'm in Orly Airport, Paris. I have been in Africa to see its need. Mauritania has especially gripped me. Now I'm hurrying home to rally help, to plead for food and funds.

But I have just missed a plane. I'll have to stay overnight. Apparently my pilot-companion and I will lose valuable time.

"Well, Lord," I sigh, "guess I can't complain. Your timing has been so perfect these past few weeks."

I wait. I pray. Yes, "This poor man cried to the Lord."

Eventually a bus appears. A bus—just for my pilot-buddy, Hank, and me? Just for the two of us? No, just before the bus pulls out, an African gentleman hurries aboard.

"You have come far?" he asks. "From Mauritania," we answer, "place called Novakchott."

He whirls around in delight and astonishment. "Then you must be Dr. Larry Ward of Food for the Hungry. I missed you in my country, and wondered as I flew here today how I could contact you. I am the Ambassador of Mauritania to the United States. I want to talk with you about the needs of our country, and how you can help!''

So the three of us—just the three of us aboard that big bus—had our private conference.

Yes, this poor man cried in Paris . . . and time was saved, not lost. Hundreds of thousands of pounds of food were rushed to desperately needy people in Mauritania, because of that "chance" meeting with a very remarkable man, the distinguished ambassador.

Saigon, 1975. There is no way I can relate the full story of the most incredible adventure of my life in this one section of one chapter.

So I'll skip over the wild-but-wonderful story of those last days of April 1975.

I was there for relief purposes, and God gave us incredible service opportunities, especially among the thousands of "Montagnards" (mountain tribes from the Central Highlands) who had fled to the Saigon area.

But that's another story. So, I reluctantly conclude, is the other story: of my escape from Vietnam with my beloved friend Garth Hunt, Asia Director of Living Bibles International—*and* over 1800 Vietnamese whom we were privileged to escort on their dash to freedom.

Let me just skip over that.

Skip over that irony of my being a fugitive from the law (from crooked elements of the South Vietnamese police, that is) in a country I have loved for almost twenty years and where I have enjoyed the finest relationships with government officials.

Skip over the memory of that wild night as I raced down the street where shots were being fired, trying to rescue a distinguished American friend who was being illegally held after trying to help some Vietnamese friends escape.

Skip over all the miracles God performed to help us leave Vietnam with that large group of deserving people (the only group of its kind).

And skip over the crazy spectacle of that gaudily-painted city bus Garth and I used to "crash the gate" at Tan Son Nhut Airbase with seventy refugees aboard. (They could turn back the military jeeps and the official Mercedes. They just didn't know how to handle that bus, with two noisy Americans shouting in a confusing mixture of Vietnamese and English and waving official-looking documents in the air!)

No, I'll just excerpt one little miracle out of many to tell you how "this poor man cried" in Vietnam.

Garth and I are in Guam, with 341 refugees in one big group. We have carefully explained why we are trying to keep our group together—so that in the United States, at this uncertain hour in human history and in the American economy, we can help them find gainful employment and have a significant new life opportunity.

The young lieutenant listens, then shakes his head sadly. "There's no way we can do it," he says. "The flights are all scheduled days in advance, and the refugees are processed individually. There's just no way to handle a group. I'm sorry."

As he walks away, someone says: "Let's call President Ford."

Someone else says, "Let's call Billy Graham."

"Men," I said, "God Himself has brought us to this point. We have seen the miracle of His provision and perfect timing. Let's just trust Him!"

Fifteen minutes later that same lieutenant bursts into the barracks where we are staying, all out of breath.

"Can you get your group together in fifteen minutes?"

"They're all together!" (By faith Garth has already assembled them.)

A little later, the last of these refugees has boarded the bus to go out to the plane which will carry them to their new life of opportunity in the United States.

I'm the last to board the bus, and I pause for just a moment to thank the young lieutenant.

"Aw, I was just doing my duty," he says.

"No," I insist, "you did more—and I thank you on behalf of all these people."

He hesitates, and then adds, almost shyly: "I—I'm glad I could help. I guess I know how they feel. I . . . was a prisoner in North Vietnam."

Guatemala, 1975: Let me tell it as simply and concisely as I can, and let the facts speak for themselves:

On February 4, 1975, Guatemala City was hit with one of the most devastating earthquakes in human history.

Three weeks earlier, on January 14, I had met in Guatemala with Capt. Jose Umberto Fuentes Soria and his associates in disaster relief coordination.

"What plan do you have," I asked, "against the threat of a major earthquake or volcanic eruption?"

Well, they *did* have a plan. A good one. We saw how we could cooperate with them if sudden disaster should come, and that same day—January 14—appointed Rev. Isai Calderon to be director of Food for the Hungry/Guatemala.

Three weeks later the earthquake ripped Guatemala in all its fury. Thank God we had already shipped 65,624 pounds of food; already had established top-level contacts; already had our own infrastructure so we could put our relief goods in honest Christian hands for effective person-to-person distribution.

Even *before* "this poor man cried, the Lord heard him"! Where do we go from here?

Yes, for the past five years especially, I have seen God's perfect timing, the incredible synchronization of His purposes.

Why? Well, "to God be the glory." All the glory. I don't want to relate all this in a way which even unconsciously may glorify self, or exploit the dramatic element.

I desperately want God to be pleased. I want Him to keep His hand on our work, to continue to direct my steps (and stops) with His perfect timing.

And I guess I know now why He has listened and responded so graciously these past five years when "this poor man cried."

I find it in His Word: "Feed the hungry! Help those in trouble! Then your light will shine out from the darkness . . . *and the Lord will guide you continually*" (Isaiah 58:10, 11).